14.2.98

For Ashley,

Kate

FAVOURITE LOVE POEMS

FAVOURITE LOVE POEMS

Chosen By

CHARLES OSBORNE

Illustrations by Robert Anning Bell

MICHAEL O'MARA BOOKS LIMITED

First published in Great Britain in 1988 by
Michael O'Mara Books Ltd,
Tremadoc Road,
London SW4 7NQ

British Library Cataloguing in Publication Data

Favourite love poems.
  1. Poetry in English.   Special subjects:
Love – Anthologies
I. Osborne, Charles, *1927–*
821'.008'0354

ISBN 1 86019 167 3

Designed by Design 23
Filmset by DP Photosetting, Aylesbury, Bucks
Printed and bound in Great Britain by
BPC Hazell Books Ltd
A member of
The British Printing Company Ltd

CONTENTS

CONTENTS

CONTENTS

CONTENTS

CONTENTS

CONTENTS

SIR THOMAS WYATT

c. 1503–1542

Remembrance

They flee from me that sometime did me seek
With naked foot stalking in my chamber.
I have seen them gentle, tame and meek,
That now are wild and do not remember
That sometime they put themself in danger
To take bread at my hand; and now they range,
Busily seeking with a continual change.

Thanked be fortune, it hath been otherwise
Twenty times better; but once in special,
In thin array after a pleasant guise,
When her loose gown from her shoulders did fall,
And she me caught in her arms long and small;
Therewithal sweetly did me kiss,
And softly said, Dear heart, how like you this?

It was no dream: I lay broad waking,
But all is turned thorough my gentleness
Into a strange fashion of forsaking;
And I have leave to go of her goodness,
And she also to use newfangleness.
But since that I so kindly am served,
I would fain know what she hath deserved.

An Appeal

And wilt thou leave me thus?
Say nay! say nay! for shame,
To save thee from the blame
Of all my grief and grame.
And wilt thou leave me thus?
Say nay! say nay!

And wilt thou leave me thus,
That hath loved thee so long
In wealth and woe among:
And is thy heart so strong
As for to leave me thus?
Say nay! say nay!

And wilt though leave me thus,
That hath given thee my heart
Never for to depart
Neither for pain nor smart:
And wilt thou leave me thus?
Say nay! say nay!

And wilt thou leave me thus,
And have no more pity
Of him that loveth thee?
Alas! thy cruelty!
And wilt thou leave me thus?
Say nay! say nay!

What Means This?

What means this? When I lie alone,
I toss, I turn, I sigh, I groan;
My bed me seems as hard as stone:
      What means this?

I sigh, I plain continually;
The clothes that on my bed do lie
Always methinks they lie awry:
    What means this?

In slumbers oft for fear I quake;
For heat and cold I burn and shake;
For lack of sleep my head doth ache:
    What means this?

A-mornings then when I do rise
I turn unto my wonted guise;
All day after muse and devise
    What means this?

And if perchance by me there pass
She unto whom I sue for grace,
The cold blood forsaketh my face:
    What means this?

But if I sit near her by,
With loud voice my heart doth cry,
And yet my mouth is dumb and dry:
    What means this?

To ask for help no heart I have,
My tongue doth fail what I should crave,
Yet inwardly I rage and rave:
    What means this?

Thus have I passed many a year
And many a day, tho naught appear;
But most of that that I most fear:
    What means this?

EDMUND SPENSER

c. 1552–1599

My Love Is Like to Ice

My love is like to ice, and I to fire:
How comes it then that this her cold so great
Is not dissolved through my so hot desire,
But harder grows the more I her entreat?
Or how comes it that my exceeding heat
Is not allayed by her heart-frozen cold,
But that I burn much more in boiling sweat,
And feel my flames augmented manifold?
What more miraculous thing may be told,
That fire, which all things melts, should harden ice,
And ice, which is congeal'd with senseless cold,
Should kindle fire by wonderful device?
Such is the power of love in gentle mind,
That it can alter all the course of kind.

One Day I Wrote Her Name Upon The Strand

One day I wrote her name upon the strand,
  But came the waves and washed it away:
  Again I wrote it with a second hand,
  But came the tide, and made my pains his prey.
'Vain man,' said she, 'thou do'st in vain assay,
  A mortal thing so to immortalize,
For I myself shall like to this decay,
  And eek my name be wiped out likewise.'
'Not so,' quoth I, 'let baser things devise
  To die in dust, but you shall live by fame:
My verse your virtues rare shall eternize,
  And in the heavens write your glorious name,
    Where, whenas death shall all the world subdue,
    Our love shall live, and later life renew.'

SIR PHILIP SIDNEY
1554–1586

The Bargain

My true love hath my heart, and I have his,
    By just exchange, one for the other given.
I hold his dear, and mine he cannot miss,
    There never was a better bargain driven.
His heart in me keeps me and him in one,
    My heart in him his thoughts and senses
    guides;
He loves my heart, for once it was his own,
    I cherish his, because in me it bides.
His heart his wound received from my sight,
    My heart was wounded with his wounded
    heart;
For as from me on him his hurt did light,
    So still methought in me his hurt did smart.
      Both equal hurt, in this change sought our
      bliss:
      My true love hath my heart and I have his.

Only Joy, Now Here You Are

Only joy, now here you are,
Fit to hear and ease my care;
Let my whispering voice obtain
Sweet reward for sharpest pain;
Take me to thee, and thee to me.
No, no, no, no, my dear, let be.

Night hath closed all in her cloak,
Twinkling stars love-thoughts provoke,
Danger hence good care doth keep,
Jealousy itself doth sleep;
Take me to thee, and thee to me.
No, no, no, no, my dear, let be.

Better place no wit can find,
Cupid's yoke to loose or bind;
These sweet flowers on fine bed too
Us in their best language woo;
Take me to thee, and thee to me.
No, no, no, no, my dear, let be.

This small light the moon bestows
Serves thy beams but to disclose;
So to raise my hap more high,
Fear not, else none can us spy;
Take me to thee, and thee to me.
No, no, no, no, my dear, let be.

That you heard was but a mouse,
Dumb sleep holdeth all the house;
Yet asleep, methinks, they say,
Young folks, take time while you may;
Take me to thee, and thee to me.
No, no, no, no, my dear, let be.

Niggard Time threats, if we miss
This large offer of our bliss,
Long stay ere he grant the same;
Sweet, then, while each thing doth frame,
Take me to thee, and thee to me.
No, no, no, no, my dear, let be.

Your fair mother is a-bed,
Candles out and curtains spread;
She thinks you do letters write;
Write, but let me first indite;
Take me to thee, and thee to me.
No, no, no, no, my dear, let be.

Sweet, alas, why strive you thus?
Concord better fitteth us;
Leave to Mars the force of hands,
Your power in your beauty stands;
Take thee to me, and me to thee.
No, no, no, no, my dear, let be.

Woe to me, and do you swear
Me to hate? but I forbear;
Cursed be my destines all,
That brought me so high to fall;
Soon with my death I will please thee.
No, no, no, no, my dear, let be.

He That Loves

He that loves and fears to try,
Learns his mistress to deny.
Doth she chide thee? 'tis to show it
That thy coldness makes her do it.
Is she silent, is she mute?
Silence fully grants thy suit.
Doth she pout and leave the room?
Then she goes to bid thee come.

Is she sick? why then be sure
She invites thee to the cure.
Doth she cross thy suit with "No"?
Tush! she loves to hear thee woo.
Doth she call the faith of men
In question? nay, she loves thee then,
And if e'er she makes a blot,
She's lost if that thou hit'st her not.

He that after ten denials
Doth attempt no further trials,
Hath no warrant to acquire
The dainties of his chaste desire.

MICHAEL DRAYTON
1563-1631

Sonnet

Since there's no help, come, let us kiss and part,
Nay, I have done: you get no more of me,
And I am glad, yea glad with all my heart,
That thus so cleanly, I myself can free.
Shake hands for ever, cancel all our vows,
And, when we meet at any time again,
Be it not seen in either of our brows
That we one jot of former love retain.
Now at the last gasp of Love's latest breath,
When, his pulse failing, passion speechless lies,
When Faith is kneeling by his bed of death,
And Innocence is closing up his eyes,
    Now if thou wouldst, when all have given him over,
    From death to life, thou might'st him yet recover.

To His Coy Love

I pray thee leave, love me no more,
    Call home the heart you gave me,
I but in vain that saint adore,
    That can, but will not save me.
These poor half kisses kill me quite;
    Was ever man thus servèd?
Amidst an ocean of delight
    For pleasure to be starvèd.

Show me no more those snowy breasts
    With azure riverets branchèd,
Where, whilst mine eyes with plenty feasts,
    Yet is my thirst not stanchèd.
O Tantalus, thy pains ne'er tell,
    By me thou art prevented,
'Tis nothing to be plagued in hell,
    But thus in heaven tormented.

Clip me no more in those dear arms,
    Nor thy life's comfort call me;
O, these are but too pow'rful charms,
    And do but more enthral me.
But see, how patient I am grown,
    In all this coil about thee;
Come, nice thing, let my heart alone,
    I cannot live without thee.

WILLIAM SHAKESPEARE
1564-1616

Sonnet 18

Shall I compare thee to a summer's day?
Thou art more lovely and more temperate.
Rough winds do shake the darling buds of May,
And summer's lease hath all too short a date.
Sometime too hot the eye of heaven shines,
And often is his gold complexion dimmed;
And every fair from fair sometime declines,
By chance, or nature's changing course,
    untrimmed;
But thy eternal summer shall not fade,
Nor lose possession of that fair thou ow'st,
Nor shall Death brag thou wand'rest in his shade,
When in eternal lines to time thou grow'st.
  So long as men can breathe or eyes can see,
  So long lives this, and this gives life to thee.

Sonnet 20

A woman's face with Nature's own hand painted,
Hast thou, the Master Mistress of my passion;
A woman's gentle heart, but not acquainted
With shifting change, as is false women's fashion;
An eye more bright than theirs, less false in rolling,
Gilding the object whereupon it gazeth;
A man in hue, all hues in his controlling,
Which steals men's eyes and women's souls amazeth.
And for a woman wert thou first created;
Till Nature, as she wrought thee, fell a-doting,
And by addition me of thee defeated
By adding one thing to my purpose nothing.
  But since she prick'd thee out for women's pleasure,
  Mine be thy love, and thy love's use their treasure.

Sonnet 29

When, in disgrace with Fortune and men's eyes,
I all alone beweep my outcast state,
And trouble deaf heaven with my bootless cries,
And look upon myself and curse my fate,
Wishing me like to one more rich in hope,
Featured like him, like him with friends
    possessed,
Desiring this man's art, and that man's scope,
With what I most enjoy contented least;
Yet in these thoughts myself almost despising,
Haply I think on thee, and then my state,
Like to the lark at break of day arising
From sullen earth, sings hymns at heaven's gate;
    For thy sweet love remember'd such wealth
    brings,
    That then I scorn to change my state with kings.

Sonnet 116

Let me not to the marriage of true minds
Admit impediments; love is not love
Which alters when it alteration finds,
Or bends with the remover to remove.
O, no, it is an ever-fixèd mark
That looks on tempests and is never shaken;
It is the star to every wand'ring bark,
Whose worth's unknown, although his height be
   taken.
Love's not Time's fool, though rosy lips and
   cheeks,
Within his bending sickle's compass come;
Love alters not with his brief hours and weeks,
But bears it out even to the edge of doom.
   If this be error and upon me proved,
   I never writ, nor no man ever loved.

Who Is Silvia?

Who is Silvia? What is she,
  That all our swains commend her,
Holy, fair, and wise is she:
  The heavens such grace did lend her,
That she might admired be.

Is she kind as she is fair?
  For beauty lives with kindness.
Love doth to her eyes repair
  To help him of his blindness,
And, being helped, inhabits there.

Then to Silvia let us sing,
  That Silvia is excelling;
She excels each mortal thing
  Upon the dull earth dwelling:
To her let us garlands bring.

CHRISTOPHER MARLOWE

1564–1593

The Passionate Shepherd to his Love

Come live with me and be my Love,
And we will the pleasures prove
That hills and valleys, dale and field,
And all the craggy mountains yield.

There will we sit upon the rocks
And see the shepherds feed their flocks,
By shallow rivers, to whose falls
Melodious birds sing madrigals.

There will I make thee beds of roses
And a thousand fragrant posies,
A cap of flowers, and a kirtle
Embroider'd all with leaves of myrtle.

A gown made of the finest wool,
Which from our pretty lambs we pull,
Fair linèd slippers for the cold,
With buckles of the purest gold.

A belt of straw and ivy buds
With coral clasps and amber studs:
And if these pleasures may thee move,
Come live with me and be my Love.

The shepherd swains shall dance and sing
For thy delight each May-morning:
If these delights thy mind may move,
Then live with me and be my Love.

SIR WALTER RALEGH

1552?–1618

The Nymph's Reply to the Shepherd

If all the world and love were young,
And truth in every shepherd's tongue,
These pretty pleasures might me move
To live with thee and be thy Love.

But Time drives flocks from field to fold;
When rivers rage and rocks grow cold;
And Philomel becometh dumb;
The rest complains of cares to come.

The flowers do fade, and wanton fields
To wayward Winter reckoning yields:
A honey tongue, a heart of gall,
Is fancy's spring, but sorrow's fall.

Thy gowns, thy shoes, thy beds of roses,
Thy cap, thy kirtle, and thy posies,
Soon break, soon wither – soon forgotten,
In folly ripe, in reason rotten.

Thy belt of straw and ivy-buds,
Thy coral clasps and amber studs, –
All these in me no means can move
to come to thee and be thy Love.

But could youth last, and love still breed,
Had joys no date, nor age no need,
Then these delights my mind might move
To live with thee and be thy Love.

Shall I Like a Hermit Dwell?

Shall I like a hermit dwell,
On a rock, or in a cell,
Calling home the smallest part
That is missing of my heart,
To bestow it where I may
Meet a rival every day?
If she undervalue me,
What care I how fair she be?

Were her tresses angel gold,
If a stranger may be bold,
Unrebuked, unafraid,
To convert them to a braid,
And with little more ado
Work them into bracelets too?
If the mine be grown so free,
What care I how rich it be?

Were her hand as rich a prize
As her hairs, or precious eyes,
If she lay them out to take
Kisses, for good manners' sake:
And let every lover skip
From her hand unto her lip;
If she seem not chaste to me,
What care I how chaste she be?

No; she must be perfect snow,
In effect as well as show;
Warming, but as snowballs do,
Not like fire, by burning too;
But when she by change hath got
To her heart a second lot,
Then if others share with me,
Farewell her, whate'er she be!

Walsinghame

As you came from the holy land
  Of Walsinghame,
Met you not with my true love
  By the way as you came?

How shall I know your true love,
  That have met many one
As I went to the holy land,
  That have come, that have gone?

She is neither white nor brown,
  But as the heavens fair:
There is none hath a form so divine
  In the earth or the air.

Such a one did I meet, good Sir,
  Such an angelic face,
Who like a queen, like a nymph, did appear,
  By her gait, by her grace.

She hath left me here all alone,
  All alone as unknown,
Who sometimes did me lead with herself,
  And me lov'd as her own.

What's the cause that she leaves you alone
  And a new way doth take,
Who loved you once as her own,
  And her joy did you make?

I have lov'd her all my youth,
  But now old as you see,
Love likes not the falling fruit
  From the withered tree:

Know that Love is a careless child,
   And forgets promise past;
He is blind, he is deaf when he list
   And in faith never fast:

His desire is a dureless content
   And a trustless joy;
He is won with a world of despair
   And is lost with a toy:

Of womenkind such indeed is the love
   Or the word love abused,
Under which many childish desires
   And conceits are excused:

But love is a durable fire,
   In the mind ever burning:
Never sick, never old, never dead,
   From itself never turning.

THOMAS CAMPION
1567–1620

Sleep, Angry Beauty

Sleep, angry beauty, sleep and fear not me:
   For who a sleeping lion dares provoke?
It shall suffice me here to sit and see
   Those lips shut up that never kindly spoke.
What sight can more content a lover's mind
Than beauty seeming harmless, if not kind?

My words have charmed her, for secure she sleeps;
   Though guilty much of wrong done to my love;
And in her slumber, see, she close-eyed, weeps!
   Dreams often more than waking passions move.
Plead, Sleep, my cause, and make her soft like thee,
That she in peace may wake and pity me.

Shall I Come, Sweet Love?

Shall I come, sweet Love, to thee
   When the evening beams are set?
Shall I not excluded be,
   Will you find no feigned let?
Let me not, for pity, more
Tell the long hours at your door.

Who can tell what thief or foe,
   In the covert of the night,
For his prey will work my woe,
   Or through wicked foul despite?
So may I die unredrest
Ere my long love be possest.

But to let such dangers pass,
   Which a lover's thoughts disdain,
'Tis enough in such a place
   To attend love's joys in vain:
Do not mock me in thy bed,
While these cold nights freeze me dead.

It Fell On A Summer's Day

It fell on a summer's day,
While sweet Bessy sleeping lay
In her bower on her bed,
Light with curtains shadowèd,
Jamie came; she him spies,
Opening half her heavy eyes.

Jamie stole in through the door,
She lay slumbering as before,
Softly to her he drew near;
She heard him, but would not hear.
Bessy vowed not to speak;
He resolved that dump to break.

First a soft kiss he did take;
She lay still and would not wake.
Then his hands learned to woo;
She dreamt not what he would do,
But still slept, while he smiled
To see love by sleep beguiled.

Jamie then began to play;
Bessy as one buried lay,
Gladly still through this sleight
Deceivèd in her own deceit.
And since this trance begun,
She sleeps every afternoon.

I Care Not For These Ladies

I care not for these ladies that must be woo'd and pray'd:
Give me kind Amaryllis, the wanton country maid.
Nature Art disdaineth; her beauty is her own.
Here when we court and kiss, she cries, "forsooth, let go!"
But when we come where comfort is, she never will say no.

If I love Amaryllis, she gives me fruit and flowers:
But if we love these ladies, we must give golden showers.
Give them gold that sell love, give me the nut-brown lass,
Who when we court and kiss she cries, "Forsooth, let go!"
But when we come where comfort is, she never will say no.

These ladies must have pillows and beds by strangers
   wrought.
Give me a bower of willows, of moss and leaves unbought,
And fresh Amaryllis with milk and honey fed;
Who when we court and kiss she cries, "Forsooth, let go!"
But when we come where comfort is, she never will say no.

Silly Boy, 'Tis Full Moon Yet

Silly boy, 'tis full moon yet, thy night as day shines clearly;
Had thy youth but wit to fear, thou couldst not love so
dearly.
Shortly wilt thou mourn when all thy pleasures are bereaved;
Little knows he how to love that never was deceived.

This is thy first maiden flame, that triumphs yet unstained;
All is artless now you speak, not one word yet is fained;
All is heav'n that you behold, and all your thoughts are
blessed:
But no Spring can want his Fall, each Troilus hath his
Cressid.

Thy well-order'd locks ere long shall rudely hang neglected;
And thy lively pleasant cheer read grief on earth dejected.
Much then wilt thou blame thy Saint, that made thy heart so
holy,
And with sighs confess, in love, that too much faith is folly.

Yet, be just and constant still; Love may beget a wonder,
Not unlike a Summer's frost, or Winter's fatal thunder:
He that holds his sweetheart true unto his day of dying
Lives, of all that ever breath'd, most worthy the envying.

SIR HENRY WOTTON

1568-1639

On His Mistress, The Queen Of Bohemia

You meaner beauties of the night,
   That poorly satisfy our eyes
More by your number than your light,
   You common people of the skies;
   What are you when the moon shall rise?

You curious chanters of the wood,
   That warble forth Dame Nature's lays,
Thinking your passions understood
   By your weak accents; what's your praise,
   When Philomel her voice shall raise?

You violets that first appear,
   By your pure purple mantles known
Like the proud virgins of the year,
   As if the spring were all your own;
   What are you when the rose is blown?

So, when my mistress shall be seen
   In form and beauty of her mind,
By virtue first, then choice, a Queen,
   Tell me if she were not designed
   Th' eclipse and glory of her kind?

THOMAS MIDDLETON

c. 1570–1627

My Love And I Must Part

Weep eyes, break heart!
  My love and I must part.
Cruel fates true love do soonest
  sever;
O, I shall see thee never, never,
  never!
O, happy is the maid whose life takes end
Ere it knows parent's frown or loss of friend!
Weep eyes, break heart!
My love and I must part.

JOHN DONNE
1572-1631

The Indifferent

    I can love both fair and brown,
Her whom abundance melts, and her whom want betrays,
Her who loves loneness best, and her who masks and plays,
    Her whom the country formed, and whom the town,
      Her who believes, and her who tries,
      Her who still weeps with spongy eyes,
    And her who is dry cork, and never cries;
    I can love her, and her, and you and you,
    I can love any, so she be not true.

    Will no other vice content you?
Will it not serve your turn to do, as did your mothers?
Or have you old vices spent, and now would find out
    others?
    Or doth a fear, that men are true, torment you?

    Oh we are not, be not you so,
    Let me, and do you, twenty know.
    Rob me, but bind me not, and let me go.
    Must I, who came to travail thorough you,
    Grow your fixed subject, because you are true?

    Venus heard me sigh this song,
And by Love's sweetest part, variety, she swore,
She heard not this till now; and vowed it should be so no
    more.
    She went, examined, and returned ere long,
      And said, alas, some two or three
      Poor heretics in love there be,
    Which think to stablish dangerous constancy.
    But I have told them, since you will be true,
    You shall be true to them, who are false to you.

The Good-Morrow

I wonder by my troth, what thou and I
   Did, till we loved? were we not weaned till then?
But sucked on country pleasures, childishly?
   Or snorted we i'the seven sleepers' den?
'Twas so; But this, all pleasures fancies be.
   If ever any beauty I did see,
Which I desired, and got, 'twas but a dream of thee.

And now good morrow to our waking souls,
   Which watch not one another out of fear;
For love, all love of other sights controls,
   And makes one little room, an everywhere.
   Let sea-discoverers to new worlds have gone,
   Let maps to others, worlds on worlds have shown,
Let us possess our world, each hath one, and is one.

   My face in thine eye, thine in mine appears,
      And true plain hearts do in the faces rest,
   Where can we find two better hemispheres
      Without sharp North, without declining West?
   Whatever dies, was not mixed equally;
   If our two loves be one, or, thou and I
Love so alike, that none do slacken, none can die.

JOHN DONNE

Love's Deity

I long to talk with some old lover's ghost,
   Who died before the God of Love was born:
I cannot think that he, who then lov'd most,
   Sunk so low, as to love one which did scorn.
But since this god produc'd a destiny,
And that vice-nature, custom, lets it be,
   I must love her, that loves not me.

Sure, they which made him god, meant not so much,
   Nor he, in his young godhead practis'd it;
But when an even flame two hearts did touch,
   His office was indulgently to fit
Actives to passives. Correspondency
Only his subject was; it cannot be
   Love, till I love her, that loves me.

But every modern god will now extend
   His vast prerogative, as far as Jove.
To rage, to lust, to write to, to commend,
   All is the purlieu of the God of Love.
Oh were we waken'd by this tyranny
To ungod this child again, it could not be
   I should love her, who loves not me.

Rebel and atheist too, why murmur I,
   As though I felt the worst that love could do?
Love might make me leave loving, or might try
   A deeper plague, to make her love me too,
Which, since she loves before, I am loth to see;
Falsehood is worse than hate; and that must be,
   If she whom I love, should love me.

JOHN DONNE

Take Heed Of Loving Me

Take heed of loving me;
At least remember I forbade it thee;
Not that I shall repair my unthrifty waste
    Of breath and blood, upon thy sighs and tears,
By being to thee then what to me thou wast;
    But so great joy our life at once outwears.
Then, lest thy love by my death frustrate be,
If thou love me, take heed of loving me.

Take heed of hating me,
Or too much triumph in the victory;
Not that I shall be mine own officer,
    And hate with hate again retaliate;
But thou wilt lose the style of conqueror,
    If I, thy conquest, perish by thy hate,
Then, lest my being nothing lessen thee,
If thou hate me, take heed of hating me.

Yet, love and hate me too;
So these extremes shall neither's office do;
Love me, that I may die the gentler way;
    Hate me, because thy love is too great for me;
Or let these two, themselves, not me, decay;
    So shall I live thy stage, not triumph be.
Lest thou thy love and hate and me undo,
To let me live, oh, love and hate me too!

JOHN DONNE

The Apparition

When by thy scorn, O murd'ress, I am dead,
   And that thou thinkst thee free
From all solicitation from me,
Then shall my ghost come to thy bed,
And thee, fain'd vestal, in worse arms shall see;
Then thy sick taper will begin to wink,
And he, whose thou art then, being tir'd before,
Will, if thou stir, or pinch to wake him, think
   Thou call'st for more,
And in false sleep will from thee shrink,
And then poor aspen wretch, neglected thou
Bath'd in a cold quicksilver sweat wilt lie
A verier ghost than I;
What I will say, I will not tell thee now,
Lest that preserve thee; and since my love is spent,
I had rather thou shouldst painfully repent,
Than by my threat'nings rest still innocent.

On Going To Bed

Come, Madam, come, all rest my powers defy,
Until I labour, I in labour lie.
The foe oft-times, having the foe in sight,
Is tired with standing, though they never fight.
Off with that girdle, like heaven's zone glistering
But a far fairer world encompassing.
Unpin that spangled breast-plate, which you wear
That th'eyes of busy fools may be stopped there:
Unlace yourself, for that harmonious chime
Tells me from you that now 'tis your bed time.
Off with that happy busk, whom I envy
That still can be, and still can stand so nigh.
Your gown's going off such beauteous state reveals
As when from flowery meads th'hills shadow steals.
Off with your wiry coronet and show
The hairy diadem which on you doth grow.
Off with those shoes: and then safely tread
In this love's hallowed temple, this soft bed.
In such white robes heaven's angels used to be
Received by men; thou Angel bring'st with thee
A heaven like Mahomet's Paradise; and though
Ill spirits walk in white, we easily know
By this these Angels from an evil sprite:
They set our hairs, but these our flesh upright.
    Licence my roving hands, and let them go
Behind, before, above, between, below.
Oh my America, my new found land,
My kingdom, safeliest when with one man manned,
My mine of precious stones, my Empery,
How blessed am I in this discovering thee.
To enter in these bonds is to be free,
Then where my hand is set my seal shall be.
    Full nakedness, all joys are due to thee.

As souls unbodied, bodies unclothed must be
To taste whole joys. Gems which you women use
Are as Atlanta's balls, cast in men's views,
That when a fool's eye lighteth on a gem
His earthly soul may covet theirs not them.
Like pictures, or like books' gay coverings made
For laymen, are all women thus arrayed;
Themselves are mystic books, which only we
Whom their imputed grace will dignify
Must see revealed. Then since I may know,
As liberally as to a midwife show
Thyself; cast all, yea this white linen hence.
Here is no penance, much less innocence.
  To teach thee, I am naked first: Why then
What need'st thou have more covering than a man.

The Ecstasy

Where, like a pillow on a bed,
  A pregnant bank swelled up, to rest
The violet's reclining head,
  Sat we two, one another's best.

Our hands were firmly cemented
  With a fast balm, which thence did spring;
Our eye-beams twisted, and did thread
  Our eyes upon one double string;

So to entergraft our hands, as yet
  Was all our means to make us one.
And pictures on our eyes to get
  Was all our propagation.

As 'twixt two equal armies, Fate
  Suspends uncertain victory,
Our souls (which to advance their state
  Were gone out) hung 'twixt her and me.

And whilst our souls negotiate there,
  We like sepulchral statues lay;
All day the same our postures were,
  And we said nothing all the day.

If any, so by love refined
  That he soul's language understood,
And by good love were grown all mind,
  Within convenient distance stood,

He (though he knew not which soul spake,
  Because both meant, both spake the same)
Might thence a new concoction take,
  And part far purer than he came.

This ecstasy doth unperplex
   (We said) and tell us what we love,
We see by this, it was not sex,
   We see, we saw not what did move:

But as all several souls contain
   Mixture of things, they know not what,
Love these mixed souls doth mix again,
   And makes both one, each this and that.

A single violet transplant,
   The strength, the colour, and the size,
(All which before was poor and scant)
   Redoubles still, and multiplies.

When love with one another so
   Interinanimates two souls,
That abler soul, which thence doth flow,
   Defects of loneliness controls.

We then, who are this new soul, know
   Of what we are composed, and made,
For the atomies of which we grow
   Are souls, whom no change can invade.

But, O alas! so long, so far
   Our bodies why do we forbear?
They are ours, though they are not we; we are
   The intelligences, they the sphere.

We owe them thanks, because they thus
   Did us, to us, at first convey,
Yielded their forces, sense, to us,
   Nor are dross to us, but allay.

On man heaven's influence works not so,
  But that it first imprints the air;
So soul into the soul may flow,
  Though it to body first repair.

As our blood labours to beget
  Spirits, as like souls as it can;
Because such fingers need to knit
  That subtle knot, which makes us man;

So must pure lovers' souls descend
  To affections, and to faculties,
Which sense may reach and apprehend,
  Else a great Prince in prison lies.

To our bodies turn we then, that so
  Weak men on love revealed may look;
Love's mysteries in souls do grow,
  But yet the body is his book.

And if some lover, such as we,
  Have heard this dialogue of one,
Let him still mark us, he shall see
  Small change, when we're to bodies gone.

Break Of Day

Stay, O sweet, and do not rise!
The light, that shines, comes from
   thine eyes.
The day breaks not: it is my heart,
Because that you and I must part.
Stay, or else my joys will die,
And perish in their infancy.

'Tis true, 'tis day: what though it be?
O, wilt thou therefore rise from me?
Why should we rise, because 'tis light?
Did we lie down, because 'twas night?
Love, which in spite of darkness brought us hither,
Should in despite of light keep us together.

Light hath no tongue, but is all eye.
If it could speak as well as spy,
This were the worst that it could say:—
That, being well, I fain would stay,
And that I lov'd my heart and honour so,
That I would not from her, that had them, go.

Must business thee from hence remove?
O, that's the worst disease of love!
The poor, the foul, the false, love can,
Admit, but not the busied man.
He, which hath business, and makes love, doth do
Such wrong, as when a married man doth woo.

BEN JONSON

1572–1637

To Celia

Drink to me only with thine eyes,
    And I will pledge with mine;
Or leave a kiss but in the cup
    And I'll not look for wine.
The thirst that from the soul doth rise
    Doth ask a drink divine;
But might I of Jove's nectar sup,
    I would not change for thine.

I sent thee late a rosy wreath,
    Not so much honouring thee
As giving it a hope that there
    It could not wither'd be;
But thou thereon didst only breathe
    And sent'st it back to me;
Since when it grows, and smells, I swear,
    Not of itself but thee!

JOHN FLETCHER
1579-1625

Take, Oh Take Those Lips Away

Take, oh take those lips away,
  That so sweetly were forsworn,
And those eyes, the break of day,
  Lights that do mislead the morn.
But my kisses bring again,
Seals of love, but sealed in vain.

Hide, oh hide those hills of snow,
  Which thy frozen bosom bears,
On whose tops the pinks that grow
  Are yet of those that April wears.
But first set my poor heart free,
Bound in those icy chains by thee.

THOMAS FORD

c. 1580–1648

There Is A Lady

There is a lady sweet and kind,
Was never face so pleas'd my mind,
I did but see her passing by,
And yet I love her till I die.

Her gesture, motion and her smiles,
Her wit, her voice my heart beguiles,
Beguiles my heart, I know not why,
And yet I love her till I die.

Her free behaviour, winning looks,
Will make a lawyer burn his books.
I touch'd her not, alas not I,
And yet I love her till die.

Had I her fast betwixt mine arms,
Judge you that think such sports were harms,
Wert any harm? no, no, fie, fie,
For I will love her till I die.

Should I remain confined there,
So long as Phoebus in his sphere,
I to request, she to deny,
Yet would I love her till I die.

Cupid is winged and doth range,
Her country so my love doth change,
But change she earth, or change she sky,
Yet will I love her till I die.

Since First I Saw Your Face

Since first I saw your face I
    resolved
    To honour and renown you;
If now I be disdained
    I wish my heart had never
    known you.
What! I that loved, and you
    that liked,
    Shall we begin to wrangle?
No, no, no, my heart is fast
    And cannot disentangle.

The sun whose beams most glorious are,
    Rejecteth no beholder,
And your sweet beauty past compare,
    Made my poor eyes the bolder.
Where beauty moves, and wit delights
    And signs of kindness bind me,
There, oh! there, where'er I go
    I leave my heart behind me.

If I admire or praise you too much,
    That fault you may forgive me,
Or if my hands had strayed but a touch,
    Then justly might you leave me.
I asked your leave, you bade me love;
    Is't now a time to chide me?
No, no, no, I'll love you still,
    What fortune e'er betide me.

ROBERT HERRICK
1591–1674

To Virgins, to Make Much of Time

Gather ye rose-buds while ye may,
  Old Time is still a-flying:
And this same flower that smiles today,
  Tomorrow will be dying.

The glorious lamp of heaven, the Sun,
  The higher he's a-getting
The sooner will his race be run,
  And nearer he's to setting.

That age is best which is the first,
  When youth and blood are warmer;
But being spent, the worse, and worst
  Times, still succeed the former.

Then be not coy, but use your time;
  And while ye may, go marry:
For having lost but once your prime,
  You may for ever tarry.

To Daisies, Not To Shut So Soon

Shut not so soon; the dull-ey'd night
  Has not as yet begun
To make a seizure on the light,
  Or to seal up the sun.

No marigolds yet closed are;
  No shadows great appear;
Nor doth the early Shepherds' Star
  Shine like a spangle here.

Stay but till my Julia close
  Her life-begetting eye;
And let the whole world then dispose
  Itself to live or die.

The Vision

Sitting alone (as one forsook)
Close by a silver-shedding brook;
With hands held up to love, I wept;
And after sorrows spent, I slept.
Then in a vision I did see
A glorious form appear to me:
A virgin's face she had; her dress
Was like a sprightly Spartaness.
A silver bow with green silk strung
Down from her comely shoulders hung;
And as she stood, the wanton air
Dangled the ringlets of her hair.
Her legs were such Diana shows,
When tucked up she a-hunting goes;
With buskins shortened to descry
The happy dawning of her thigh:
Which when I saw, I made access
To kiss that tempting nakedness.
But she forbade me, with a wand
Of myrtle she had in her hand;
And chiding me, said, hence, remove,
Herrick, thou art too coarse to love.

ROBERT HERRICK

Upon the Nipples of Julia's Breast

Have ye beheld (with much delight)
A red rose peeping through a white?
Or else a cherry (double grac'd)
Within a lily? Centre plac'd?
Or ever mark'd the pretty beam,
A strawberry shows, half drown'd in cream?
Or seen rich rubies blushing through
A pure smooth pearl, and orient too?
So like to this, nay all the rest,
Is each neat niplet of her breast.

Julia

Some asked me where the rubies
   grew,
   And nothing did I say,
But with my finger pointed to
   The lips of Julia.

Some asked how pearls did grow, and where;
   Then spake I to my girl,
To part her lips and show me there
   The quarelets of pearl.

One asked me where the roses grew;
   I bade him not go seek,
But forthwith bade my Julia show
   A bud in either cheek.

THOMAS CAREW
1598–1639

A Song

Ask me no more where Jove bestows,
When June is past, the fading rose;
For in your beauty's orient deep
These flowers, as in their causes, sleep.

Ask me no more whither do stray
The golden atoms of the day;
For in pure love heaven did prepare
Those powders to enrich your hair.

Ask me no more whither doth haste
The nightingale, when May is past;
For in your sweet dividing throat
She winters, and keeps warm her note.

Ask me no more where those stars 'light,
That downwards fall in dead of night;
For in your eyes they sit, and there
Fixèd become, as in their sphere.

Ask me no more if east or west
The phoenix builds her spicy nest;
For unto you at last she flies,
And in your fragrant bosom dies.

ANONYMOUS
1597

Dear, If You Change

Dear, if you change, I'll never choose again;
Sweet, if you shrink, I'll never think of love;
Fair, if you fail, I'll judge all beauty vain;
Wise, if too weak, more wits I'll never prove.
　　Dear, sweet, fair, wise, change, shrink, nor be not weak;
　　And, on my faith, my faith shall never break.

Earth with her flowers shall sooner heaven adorn;
Heaven her bright stars, through earth's dim globe shall
move.
Fire, heat shall lose; and frosts of flames be born;
Air made to shine, as black as hell shall prove:
　　Earth, heaven, fire, air, the world transformed shall view,
　　Ere I prove false to faith, or strange to you.

ANONYMOUS
Western Wind

Western wind, when wilt thou blow,
The small rain down can rain?
Christ, that my love were in my arms,
And I in my bed again.

ANONYMOUS
c. 1600

Come, Pretty One

Come, pretty one, shall I love thee?
Say, little one, shall I prove thee?
Gently moving, be not cruel,
Wish lovingly, O my jewel;
Talk coyly, move affection;
Toy prettily, cause erection;
Look merrily while I woo thee,
Blush cheerfully whilst I do thee.
Look prettily, O that's meetest!
So feelingly, O that's sweetest!
Fall willingly and lie flatly,
Keep close to me whilst thou'rt at me,
Move sprightfully and lie panting,
Show rightly nothing be wanting.
Speak faintly – fairly languish –
Die daintily in sweet anguish.
Swear evermore I shall woo thee,
And evermore pluck me to thee.

EDMUND WALLER

1606–1687

Song

Go, lovely rose–
Tell her that wastes her time and me,
That now she knows,
When I resemble her to thee,
How sweet and fair she seems to be.

Tell her that's young,
And shuns to have her graces spied,
That hadst thou sprung
In deserts where no men abide,
Thou must have uncommended died.

Small is the worth
Of beauty from the light retired:
Bid her come forth,
Suffer herself to be desired,
And not blush so to be admired.

Then die! – that she
The common fate of all things rare
May read in thee;
How small a part of time they share
That are so wondrous sweet and fair!

JOHN MILTON

1608–1674

On His Deceased Wife

Methought I saw my late espoused Saint
  Brought to me like Alcestis from the grave,
Whom Jove's great Son to her glad Husband gave,
  Rescu'd from death by force though pale and faint.
Mine as whom washt from spot of child-bed taint,
  Purification in the old Law did save,
  And such, as yet once more I trust to have
  Full sight of her in Heaven without restraint,
Came vested all in white, pure as her mind:
  Her face was vail'd, yet to my fancied sight,
  Love, sweetness, goodness, in her person shin'd
So clear, as in no face with more delight.
  But O as to embrace me she enclin'd
  I wak'd, she fled, and day brought back my night.

SIR JOHN SUCKLING

1609–1642

Song

Why so pale and wan, fond lover?
   Prithee, why so pale?
Will, when looking well can't move her,
   Looking ill prevail?
   Prithee, why so pale?

Why so dull and mute, young sinner?
   Prithee, why so mute?
Will, when speaking well can't win her,
   Saying nothing do't?
   Prithee, why so mute?

Quit, quit for shame! This will not move;
   This cannot take her.
If of herself she will not love,
   Nothing can make her:
   The devil take her.

A Poem With The Answer

Out upon it, I have lov'd
   Three whole days together;
And am like to love three more,
   If it prove fair weather.

Time shall moult away his wings
   Ere he shall discover
In the whole wide world again
   Such a constant lover.

But the spite on't is, no praise
   Is due at all to me:
Love with me had made no stays
   Had it any been but she.

Had it any been but she
   And that very face,
There had been at least ere this
   A dozen dozen in her place.

ANONYMOUS

c. 1610

Love Me Little, Love Me Long

Love me little, love me long,
   Is the burden of my song;
Love that is too hot and strong
   Burneth soon to waste;
Still I would not have thee
     cold,
   Or backward, or too bold,
For love that lasteth till 'tis old
   Fadeth not in haste.

Winter's cold, or summer's heat,
   Autumn tempests on its beat,
It can never know defeat,
   Never can rebel;
Such the love that I would gain,
   Such love, I tell thee plain,
That thou must give or love in vain,
   So to thee farewell.

The Song of Solomon, Chapter 2

I am the rose of Sharon, and the lily of the valleys.

As the lily among thorns, so is my love among the daughters.

As the apple tree among the trees of the wood, so is my beloved among the sons. I sat down under his shadow with great delight, and his fruit was sweet to my taste.

He brought me to the banqueting house, and his banner over me was love.

Stay me with flagons, comfort me with apples: for I am sick of love.

His left hand is under my head, and his right hand doth embrace me.

I charge you, O yet daughters of Jerusalem, by the roes, and by the hinds of the field, that ye stir not up, nor awake my love, till he please.

The voice of my beloved! behold, he cometh leaping upon the mountains, skipping upon the hills.

My beloved is like a roe or a young hart: behold, he standeth behind our wall, he looketh forth at the windows, showing himself through the lattice.

My beloved spake, and said unto me, Rise up, my love, my fair one, and come away.

For, lo, the winter is past, the rain is over and gone;

The flowers appear on the earth; the time of the singing of birds is come, and the voice of the turtle is heard in our land:

The fig tree putteth forth her green figs, and the vines with the tender grape give a good smell. Arise, my love, my fair one, and come away.

O my dove, that art in the clefts of the rock, in the secret places of the stairs, let me see thy countenance, let me hear thy voice; for sweet is thy voice, and thy countenance is comely.

Take us the foxes, the little foxes, that spoil the vines: for our vines have tender grapes.

My beloved is mine, and I am his: he feedeth among the lilies.

Until the day break, and the shadows flee away, turn, my beloved, and be thou like a roe or a young hart upon the mountains of Bether.

WILLIAM CARTWRIGHT

1611–1643

No Platonic Love

Tell me no more of minds embracing minds,
    And hearts exchang'd for hearts;
That spirits spirits meet, as winds do winds,
    And mix their subt'lest parts;
That two unbodied essences may kiss,
And then like angels, twist and feel one bliss.

I was that silly thing that once was wrought
    To practise this thin love;
I climb'd from sex to soul, from soul to thought;
    But thinking there to move,
Headlong I roll'd from thought to soul, and then
From soul I lighted at the sex agen.

As some strict down-look'd men pretend to fast,
    Who yet in closets eat;
So lovers who profess they spirits taste,
    Feed yet on grosser meat;
I know they boast they souls to souls convey,
Howe'er they meet, the body is the way.

Come, I will undeceive thee, they that tread
    Those vain aerial ways,
Are like young heirs and alchymists misled
    To waste their wealth and days,
For searching thus to be for ever rich,
They only find a med'cine for the itch.

RICHARD LOVELACE

1618–1657

To Lucasta, Going to the Wars

Tell me not, sweet, I am unkind,
    That from the nunnery
Of thy chaste breast and quiet mind,
    To war and arms I fly.

True, a new mistress now I chase,
    The first foe in the field;
And with a stronger faith embrace
    A sword, a horse, a shield.

Yet this inconstancy is such
    As you too shall adore;
I could not love thee, dear, so much,
    Lov'd I not Honour more.

To Althea, from Prison

When Love with unconfinèd wings
    Hovers within my gates,
And my divine Althea brings
    To whisper at the grates;
When I lie tangled in her hair
    And fetter'd to her eye,
The birds that wanton in the air
    Know no such liberty.

When flowing cups run swiftly round
    With no allaying Thames,
Our careless heads with roses crown'd,
    Our hearts with loyal flames;
When thirsty grief in wine we steep,
    When healths and draughts go free—
Fishes that tipple in the deep
    Know no such liberty.

When, linnet-like confinèd, I
    With shriller throat shall sing
The sweetness, mercy, majesty
    And glories of my King;
When I shall voice aloud how good
    He is, how great should be,
Enlargèd winds, that curl the flood,
    Know no such liberty.

Stone walls do not a prison make,
    Nor iron bars a cage;
Minds innocent and quiet take
    That for an hermitage:
If I have freedom in my love
    And in my soul am free,
Angels alone, that soar above,
    Enjoy such liberty.

The Scrutiny

Why should you swear I am forsworn,
    Since thine I vowed to be?
Lady it is already morn,
    And 'twas last night I swore to thee
That fond impossibility.

Have I not loved thee much and long,
    A tedious twelve hours' space?
I must all other Beauties wrong,
    And rob thee of a new embrace;
Could I still dote upon thy face.

Not, but all joy in thy brown hair,
    By others may be found;
But I must search the black and fair
    Like skilful mineralists that sound
For treasure in un-plowed-up ground.

Then, if when I have loved my round,
    Thou provest the pleasant she;
With spoils of meaner Beauties crowned,
    I laden will return to thee,
Ev'n sated with variety.

ANDREW MARVELL
1621–1678

To His Coy Mistress

Had we but world enough, and time,
This coyness, lady, were no crime.
We would sit down, and think which way
To walk, and pass our long love's day.
Thou by the Indian Ganges' side
Should'st rubies find: I by the tide
Of Humber would complain. I would
Love you ten years before the Flood,
And you should, if you please, refuse
Till the conversion of the Jews.
My vegetable love should grow
Vaster than empires, and more slow.
An hundred years should go to praise
Thine eyes, and on thy forehead gaze:
Two hundred to adore each breast;
But thirty thousand to the rest;
An age at least to every part,
And the last age should show your heart.
For, lady, you deserve this state,
Nor would I love at lower rate.
    But at my back I always hear
Time's wingèd chariot hurrying near:
And yonder all before us lie
Deserts of vast eternity.
Thy beauty shall no more be found;
Nor, in thy marble vault, shall sound
My echoing song: then worms shall try
That long-preserved virginity,
And your quaint honour turn to dust,
And into ashes all my lust.

The grave's a fine and private place,
But none, I think, do there embrace.
   Now, therefore, while the youthful hue
Sits on thy skin like morning dew,
And while thy willing soul transpires
At every pore with instant fires,
Now let us sport us while we may;
And now, like amorous birds of prey,
Rather at once our Time devour,
Than languish in his slow-chapt power.
Let us roll all our strength and all
Our sweetness up into one ball,
And tear our pleasures with rough strife
Thorough the iron gates of life.
Thus, though we cannot make our Sun
Stand still, yet we will make him run.

ANDREW MARVELL

Definition Of Love

My Love is of a birth as rare
As 'tis for object strange and high:
It was begotten by Despair
Upon Impossibility.

Magnanimous Despair alone
Could show me so divine a thing,
Where feeble Hope could ne'er have flown
But vainly flapped its tinsel wing.

And yet I quickly might arrive
Where my extended soul is fixed,
But Fate does iron wedges drive,
And always crowds itself betwixt.

For Fate with jealous eye does see
Two perfect Loves; nor lets them close:
Their union would her ruin be,
And her tyrannic power depose.

And therefore her decrees of steel
Us as the distant Poles have placed,
(Though Love's whole World on us doth wheel)
Not by themselves to be embraced.

Unless the giddy Heaven fall,
And Earth some new convulsion tear;
And, us to join, the World should all
Be cramped into a planisphere.

As lines so Love oblique may well
Themselves in every angle greet:
But ours so truly parallel,
Though infinite, can never meet.

Therefore the Love which us doth bind
But Fate so enviously debars,
Is the conjunction of the Mind,
And opposition of the Stars..

JOHN DRYDEN

1631–1700

Love's Fancy

After the pangs of a desperate lover,
When day and night I have sigh'd all in vain,
Ah what a pleasure it is to discover
In her eyes pity, who causes my pain!

When with unkindness our love at a stand is,
And both have punish'd ourselves with the pain,
Ah what a pleasure the touch of her hand is!
Ah what a pleasure to press it again!

When the denial comes fainter and fainter,
And her eyes give what her tongue does deny,
Ah what a trembling I feel when I venture!
Ah what a trembling does usher my joy!

When 'with a sigh, she accords me the blessing,
And her eyes twinkle 'twixt pleasure and pain,
Ah what a joy 'tis, beyond all expressing!
Ah what a joy to hear, "Shall we again?"

Whilst Alexis Lay Prest

Whilst Alexis lay prest
  In her arms he loved best,
With his hands round her neck,
  And his head on her breast,
He found the fierce pleasure too hasty to stay,
And his soul in the tempest just flying away.

When Celia saw this,
With a sigh and a kiss,
She cried, "Oh, my dear, I am robbed of my bliss!
'Tis unkind to your love, and unfaithfully done,
To leave me behind you, and die all alone."

The youth, though in haste,
And breathing his last,
In pity died slowly, while she died more fast;
Till at length she cried, "Now, my dear, now let us go:
Now die, my Alexis, and I will die too!"

Thus entranced they did lie,
Till Alexis did try
To recover new breath, that again he might die:
Then often they died; but the more they did so,
The nymph died more quick, and the shepherd more slow.

THOMAS SHIPMAN

c. 1632

The Resolute Courtier

Prithee, say aye or no;
If thou'lt not have me, tell me so;
  I cannot stay,
  Nor will I wait upon
  A smile or frown.
If thou wilt have me, say;
Then I am thine, or else I am mine own.

  Be white or black; I hate
Dependence on a checkered fate;
  Let go, or hold;
  Come either kiss or not:
  Now to be hot,
  And then again as cold,
Is a fantastic fever you have got.

  A tedious woo is base,
And worse by far than a long grace:
  For whilst we stay,
  Our lingering spoils the roast,
  Or stomach's lost;
  Nor can, nor will I stay;
For if I sup not quickly, I will fast.

  Whilst we are fresh and stout
And vigorous, let us to 't:
  Alas, what good
  From wrinkled man appears,
  Gelded with years,
  When his thin wheyish blood
Is far less comfortable than his tears?

PHILIP AYRES
On Lydia Distracted

With hairs, which for the wind to play with, hung,
   With her torn garments, and with naked feet,
   Fair Lydia dancing went from street to street,
Singing with pleasant voice her foolish song.
On her she drew all eyes in ev'ry place,
   And them to pity by her pranks did move,
   Which turn'd with gazing longer into Love
By the rare beauty of her charming face.

In all her frenzies, and her mimicries,
While she did Nature's richest gifts despise,
   There active Love did subt'ly play his part.
Her antic postures made her look more gay,
Her ragged clothes her treasures did display,
   And with each motion she ensnar'd a heart.

SIR CHARLES SEDLEY

1639–1701

To Cloris

Cloris, I cannot say your eyes
Did my unwary heart surprise;
Nor will I swear it was your face,
Your shape, or any nameless grace:
For you are so entirely fair,
To love a part, injustice were;
No drowning man can know which drop
Of water his last breath did stop;
So when the stars in heaven appear,
And join to make the night look clear;
The light we no one's bounty call,
But the obliging gift of all.
He that does lips or hands adore,
Deserves them only, and no more;
But I love all, and every part,
And nothing less can ease my heart.
Cupid, that lover, weakly strikes,
Who can express what 'tis he likes.

On The Happy Corydon And Phyllis

Young Corydon and Phyllis
   Sat in a lovely grove,
Contriving crowns of lilies,
   Repeating toys of love,
And something else, but what I dare not name.

But as they were a-playing,
   She ogled so the swain;
It saved her plainly saying
   Let's kiss to ease our pain:
And something else, but what I dare not name.

A thousand times he kissed her,
   Laying her on the green;
But as he farther pressed her,
   A pretty leg was seen:
And something else, but what I dare not name.

So many beauties viewing,
   His ardour still increased;
And greater joys pursuing,
   He wandered o'er her breast:
And something else, but what I dare not name.

A last effort she trying,
   His passion to withstand;
Cried, but it was faintly crying,
   Pray take away your hand:
And something else, but what I dare not name.

Young Corydon grown bolder,
   The minutes would improve;
This is the time, he told her,
   To show you how I love;
And something else, but what I dare not name.

The nymph seemed almost dying,
 Dissolved in amorous heat;
She kissed and told him sighing,
 My dear, your love is great:
And something else, but what I dare not name.

But Phyllis did recover
 Much sooner than the swain;
She blushing asked her lover,
 Shall we not kiss again:
And something else, but what I dare not name.

Thus Love his revels keeping,
 'Til Nature at a stand;
From talk they fell to sleeping,
 Holding each others hand;
And something else, but what I dare not name.

APHRA BEHN
1640-1689

Amyntas Led Me to a Grove

Amyntas led me to a Grove,
   Where all the trees did shade us;
The Sun itself, tho it had strove,
   Yet could not have betray'd us.
The place secure from human Eyes,
   No other fear allows,
But when the Winds that gently rise
   Do kiss the yielding Boughs.

Down there we sat upon the Moss,
   And did begin to play
A thousand wanton Tricks, to pass
   The Heat of all the Day.
A many Kisses he did give,
   And I return'd the same:
Which made me willing to receive
   That which I dare not name.

His charming Eyes no aid requir'd,
   To tell their amorous Tale;
On her that was already fir'd,
   'Twas easy to prevail.
He did but kiss, and clasp me round,
   Whilst they his thoughts exprest,
And laid me gently on the Ground;
Oh! who can guess the rest?

CHARLES SACKVILLE,
EARL OF DORSET
1643–1706

The Advice

Would you in love succeed, be brisk, be gay,
Cast all dull thoughts and serious looks away;
Think not with downcast eyes, and mournful air
To move to pity the relentless Fair,
Or draw from her bright eyes a crystal tear.
This method foreign is to your affair,
Too formal for the frolic you prepare:
Thus, when you think she yields to love's advance,
You'll find 'tis no consent, but complaisance.
Whilst he who boldly rifles all her charms,
Kisses and ravishes her in his arms,
Seizes the favour, stays not for a grant,
Alarms her blood and makes her sigh and pant,
Gives her no time to speak, or think't a crime,
Enjoys his wish, and well employs his time.

JOHN WILMOT,
EARL OF ROCHESTER
1647–1680

Song

Absent from thee, I languish still;
  Then ask me not, when I return?
The straying fool 'twill plainly kill
  To wish all day, all night to mourn.

Dear! from thine arms then let me fly,
  That my fantastic mind may prove
The torments it deserves to try
  That tears my fixed heart from my love.

When, wearied with a world of woe,
  To thy safe bosom I retire
Where love and peace and truth does flow,
  May I contented there expire,

Lest, once more wandering from that heaven,
  I fall on some base heart unblest,
Faithless to thee, false, unforgiven,
  And lose my everlasting rest.

Song Of A Young Lady To Her Ancient Lover

Ancient person, for whom I
All the flattering youth defy,
Long be it ere thou grow old,
Aching, shaking, crazy, cold;
    But still continue as thou art,
    Ancient person of my heart.

On thy withered lips and dry,
Which like barren furrows lie,
Brooding kisses I will pour
Shall thy youthful heat restore
(Such kind showers in autumn fall,
And a second spring recall);
    Nor from thee will ever part,
    Ancient person of my heart.

Thy nobler part, which but to name
In our sex would be counted shame,
By age's frozen grasp possessed,
From his ice shall be released,
And soothed by my reviving hand,
In former warmth and vigor stand.
All a lover's wish can reach
For thy joy my love shall teach,
And for thy pleasure shall improve
All that art can add to love.
    Yet still I love thee without art,
    Ancient person of my heart.

Song

Love a woman? You're an ass!
 'Tis a most insipid passion
To choose out for your happiness
 The silliest part of God's creation.

Let the porter and the groom,
 Things designed for dirty slaves,
Drudge in fair Aurelia's womb
 To get supplies for age and graves.

Farewell, woman! I intend
 Henceforth every night to sit
With my lewd, well-natured friend,
 Drinking to engender wit.

Then give me health, wealth, mirth, and wine,
 And, if busy love entrenches,
There's a sweet, soft page of mine
 Does the trick worth forty wenches.

MATTHEW PRIOR
1664–1721

Phillis's Age

How old may Phillis be, you ask,
　　Whose beauty thus all hearts engages?
To answer is no easy task:
　　For she has really two ages.

Stiff in brocade, and pinch'd in stays,
　　Her patches, paint, and jewels on;
All day let envy view her face,
　　And Phillis is but twenty-one.

Paint, patches, jewels laid aside,
　　At night astronomers agree,
The evening has the day belied;
　　And Phillis is some forty-three.

SIR JOHN VANBRUGH

1664–1726

An Angelic Woman

Not an angel dwells above
Half so fair as her I love.
Heaven knows how she'll receive me:
If she smiles I'm blest indeed;
If she frowns I'm quickly
   freed;
Heaven knows she ne'er can grieve me.

None can love her more than I,
Yet she ne'er shall make me die,
If my flame can never warm her:
Lasting beauty I'll adore,
I shall never love her more,
Cruelty will so deform her.

JONATHAN SWIFT
1667–1745

Stella's Birthday

Stella this day is thirty-four,
(We shan't dispute a year or more:)
However, Stella, be not troubled,
Although thy size and years are doubled
Since first I saw thee at sixteen,
The brightest virgin on the green;
So little is thy form declined;
Made up so largely in thy mind.
   O, would it please the gods to split
Thy beauty, size, and years, and wit!
No age could furnish out a pair
Of nymphs so graceful, wise, and fair;
With half the lustre of your eyes,
With half your wit, your years, and size.
And then, before it grew too late,
How should I beg of gentle fate,
(That either nymph might have her swain,)
To split my worship too in twain.

WILLIAM CONGREVE
1670–1729

False Though She Be

False though she be to me and love,
    I'll ne'er pursue revenge;
For still the charmer I approve,
    Though I deplore her change.

In hours of bliss we oft have met;
    They could not always last:
And though the present I regret,
    I'm grateful for the past.

Pious Celinda

Pious Celinda goes to prayers,
    If I but ask the favour;
And yet the tender fool's in tears
    When she believes I'll leave her.

Would I were free from this restraint,
    Or else had hopes to win her;
Would she could make of me a saint,
    Or I of her a sinner.

ANONYMOUS

c. 1671

The Pretty, Drowsy Rogue

Last night I dreamed of my love
When sleep did overtake her.
It was a pretty, drowsy rogue;
She slept; I durst not wake her.

Her lips were like to coral red;
A thousand times I kissed 'um,
And a thousand more I might have stolen,
For she had never missed 'um.

Her crisped locks, like threads of gold,
Hung dangling o'er the pillows;
Great pity 'twas that one so fair
Should wear the rainbow-willow.

I folded down the holland sheet
A little below her belly,
But what I did you ne'er shall know,
Nor is it meet to tell ye.

Her belly's like to yonder hill –
Some call it Mount of Pleasure –
And underneath there springs a well
Which no man's depth can measure.

AMBROSE PHILIPS

1674–1749

The Happy Swain

Have ye seen the morning sky,
When the dawn prevails on high,
When, anon, some purply ray
Gives a sample of the day,
When, anon, the lark, on wing,
Strives to soar, and strains to sing?

Have ye seen th'ethereal blue
Gently shedding silvery dew,
Spangling o'er the silent green,
While the nightingale, unseen,
To the moon and stars, full bright,
Lonesome chants the hymn of night?

Have ye seen the broid'red May
All her scented bloom display,
Breezes opening, every hour,
This, and that, expecting flower,
While the mingling birds prolong,
From each bush, the vernal song?

Have ye seen the damask-rose
Her unsully'd blush disclose,
Or the lilly's dewy bell,
In her glossy white, excell,
Or a garden vary'd o'er
With a thousand glories more?

By the beauties these display,
Morning, evening, night, or day,
By the pleasures these excite,
Endless sources of delight!
Judge, by them, the joys I find,
Since my Rosalind was kind,
Since she did herself resign
To my vows, for ever mine.

HENRY CAREY

1687?–1743

Sally in our Alley

Of all the girls that are so smart
　There's none like pretty Sally;
She is the darling of my heart,
　And she lives in our alley.
There is no lady in the land
　Is half so sweet as Sally;
She is the darling of my heart,
　And she lives in our alley.

Her father he makes cabbage-nets
　And through the streets does cry'em;
Her mother she sells laces long
　To such as please to buy 'em:
But sure such folks could ne'er beget
　So sweet a girl as Sally!
She is the darling of my heart,
　And she lives in our alley.

When she is by, I leave my work,
　I love her so sincerely;
My master comes like any Turk,
　And bangs me most severely–
But let him bang his bellyful,
　I'll bear it all for Sally;
She is the darling of my heart,
　And she lives in our alley.

Of all the days that's in the week
   I dearly love but one day–
And that's the day that comes betwixt
   A Saturday and Monday;
For then I'm drest all in my best
   To walk abroad with Sally;
She is the darling of my heart,
   And she lives in our alley.

My master carries me to church,
   And often am I blamed
Because I leave him in the lurch
   As soon as text is named;
I leave the church in sermon-time
   And slink away to Sally;
She is the darling of my heart,
   And she lives in our alley.

When Christmas comes about again
   O then I shall have money;
I'll hoard it up, and box it all,
   I'll give it to my honey:
I would it were ten thousand pound,
   I'd give it all to Sally;
She is the darling of my heart,
   And she lives in our alley.

My master and the neighbours all
   Make game of me and Sally,
And, but for her, I'd better be
   A slave and row a galley;
But when my seven long years are out
   O then I'll marry Sally,–
O then we'll wed, and then we'll bed,
   But not in our alley!

JAMES THOMSON

1700–1748

Song

One day the god of fond desire,
  On mischief bent, to Damon said,
'Why not disclose your tender fire?
  Not own it to the lovely maid?'

The shepherd marked his treacherous art,
  And, softly sighing, thus replied:
''Tis true, you have subdued my heart,
  But shall not triumph o'er my pride.

'The slave in private only bears
  Your bondage, who his love conceals;
But when his passion he declares,
  You drag him at your chariot-wheels.

RICHARD BRINSLEY SHERIDAN

1751–1816

The Geranium

In the close covert of a grove,
By nature formed for scenes of love,
Said Susan in a lucky hour,
Observe yon sweet geranium flower;
How straight upon its stalk it stands,
And tempts our violating hands:
Whilst the soft bud as yet unspread,
Hangs down its pale declining head:
Yet, soon as it is ripe to blow,
The stems shall rise, the head shall glow.
Nature, said I, my lovely Sue,
To all her followers lends a clue;
Her simple laws themselves explain,
As links of one continued chain;
For her the mysteries of creation,
Are but the works of generation:
Yon blushing, strong, triumphant flower,
Is in the crisis of its power:
But short, alas! its vigorous reign,
He sheds his seed, and drops again;
The bud that hangs in pale decay,
Feels, not, as yet, the plastic ray;
Tomorrow's sun shall bid him rise,
Then, too, he sheds his seed and dies:
But words, my love, are vain and weak,
For proof, let bright example speak;
Then straight before the wondering maid,
The tree of life I gently laid;
Observe, sweet Sue, his drooping head,

How pale, how languid, and how dead;
Yet, let the sun of thy bright eyes,
Shine but a moment, it shall rise;
Let but the dew of thy soft hand
Refresh the stem, it straight shall stand:
Already, see, it swells, it grows,
Its head is redder than the rose,
Its shrivelled fruit, of dusky hue,
Now glows, a present fit for Sue:
The balm of life each artery fills,
And in o'erflowing drops distils.
Oh me! cried Susan, when is this?
What strange tumultuous throbs of bliss!
Sure, never mortal, till this hour,
Felt such emotion at a flower:
Oh, serpent! cunning to deceive,
Sure, 'tis this tree that tempted Eve;
The crimson apples hang so fair,
Alas! what woman could forbear?
Well hast thou guessed, my love, I cried,
It is the tree by which she died;
The tree which could content her,
All nature, Susan, seeks the centre;
Yet, let us still, poor Eve forgive,
It's the tree by which we live;
For lovely woman still it grows,
And in the centre only blows.
But chief for thee, it spreads its charms,
For paradise is in thy arms. –
I ceased, for nature kindly here
Began to whisper in her ear:
And lovely Sue lay softly panting,
While the geranium tree was planting.

'Til in the heat of amorous strife,
She burst the mellow tree of life.
'Oh, heaven!' cried Susan, with a sigh,
'The hour we taste – we surely die;
Strange raptures seize my fainting frame,
And all my body glows with flame;
Yet let me snatch one parting kiss
To tell my love I die with bliss:
That pleased, thy Susan yields her breath;
Oh! who would live if this be death!'

WILLIAM BLAKE

1757–1827

Never Seek to Tell Thy Love

Never seek to tell thy love
Love that never told can be;
For the gentle wind does move
Silently, invisibly.

I told my love, I told my love,
I told her all my heart,
Trembling, cold, in ghastly fears—
Ah, she did depart.

Soon as she was gone from me
A traveller came by
Silently, invisibly;
O, was no deny.

ROBERT BURNS

1759–1796

John Anderson My Jo

John Anderson my jo, John,
   When we were first acquent;
Your locks were like the raven,
   Your bony brow was brent;
But now your brow is beld, John,
   Your locks are like the snaw;
But blessings on your frosty pow,
   John Anderson my Jo.

John Anderson my jo, John,
   We clamb the hill the gither;
And mony a canty day, John,
   We've had wi' ane anither:
Now we maun totter down, John,
   And hand in hand we'll go;
And sleep the gither at the foot,
   John Anderson my Jo.

My Love is Like A Red, Red Rose

O, my luve's like a red, red rose,
    That's newly sprung in June;
O, my luve's like the melodie
    That's sweetly play'd in tune.

As fair art thou, my bonnie lass,
    So deep in luve am I;
And I will luve thee still, my dear,
    Till a' the seas gang dry

Till a' the seas gang dry, my dear,
    And the rocks melt wi' the sun;
I will luve thee still, my dear,
    While the sands of life shall run.

And fare thee weel, my only luve!
    And fare thee weel a while!
And I will come again, my luve,
    Tho' it were ten thousand mile.

WILLIAM WORDSWORTH

1770–1850

She Dwelt Among the Untrodden Ways

She dwelt among the untrodden ways
   Beside the springs of Dove,
A maid whom there were none to praise
   And very few to love:

A violet by a mossy stone
   Half hidden from the eye!
—Fair as a star, when only one
Is shining in the sky.

She lived unknown, and few could know
   When Lucy ceased to be;
But she is in her grave, and, oh,
   The difference to me!

Surprised by Joy

Surprised by joy – impatient as the wind
   I turned to share the transport – O! with whom
   But Thee, deep buried in the silent tomb,
That spot which no vicissitude can find?
Love, faithful love, recalled thee to my mind –
   But how could I forget thee? Through what power,
   Even for the least division of an hour,
Have I been so beguiled as to be blind
To my most grievous loss! – That thought's return
   Was the worst pang that sorrow ever bore,
Save one, one only, when I stood forlorn,
   Knowing my heart's best treasure was no more;
That neither present time, nor years unborn
   Could to my sight that heavenly face restore.

WILLIAM WORDSWORTH

Strange Fits of Passion

Strange fits of passion have I known:
    And I will dare to tell,
But in the Lover's ear alone,
    What once to me befell.

When she I loved looked every day
    Fresh as a rose in June,
I to her cottage bent my way,
    Beneath an evening-moon.

Upon the moon I fixed my eye,
    All over the wide lea;
With quickening pace my horse drew nigh
    Those paths so dear to me.

And now we reached the orchard-plot;
    And, as we climbed the hill,
The sinking moon to Lucy's cot
    Came near, and nearer still.

In one of those sweet dreams I slept,
    Kind Nature's gentlest boon!
And all the while my eyes I kept
    On the descending moon.

My horse moved on; hoof after hoof
    He raised, and never stopped:
When down behind the cottage roof,
    At once, the bright moon dropped.

What fond and wayward thoughts will slide
    Into a Lover's head!
'O mercy!' to myself I cried,
    'If Lucy should be dead!'

Louisa,

After Accompanying Here on a Mountain Excursion

I met Louisa in the shade,
And, having seen that lovely Maid,
Why should I fear to say
That, nymph-like, she is fleet and strong,
And down the rocks can leap along
Like rivulets in May?

And she hath smiles to earth unknown;
Smiles, that with motion of their own
Do spread, and sink, and rise;
That come and go with endless play,
And ever, as they pass away,
Are hidden in her eyes.

She loves her fire, her cottage-home;
Yet o'er the moorland will she roam
In weather rough and bleak;
And, when against the wind she strains,
Oh! might I kiss the mountain rains
That sparkle on her cheek.

Take all that's mine 'beneath the moon,'
If I with her but half a noon
May sit beneath the walls
Of some old cave, or mossy nook,
When up she winds along the brook
To hunt the waterfalls.

Among all Lovely Things My Love Had Been

Among all lovely things my Love had been;
Had noted well the stars, all flowers that grew
About her home; but she had never seen
A glow-worm, never one, and this I knew.

While riding near her home one stormy night
A single glow-worm did I chance to espy;
I gave a fervent welcome to the sight,
And from my horse I leapt; great joy had I.

Upon a leaf the glow-worm did I lay,
To bear it with me through the stormy night:
And, as before, it shone without dismay;
Albeit putting forth a fainter light.

When to the dwelling of my Love I came,
I went into the orchard quietly;
And left the glow-worm, blessing it by name,
Laid safely by itself, beneath a tree.

The whole next day, I hoped, and hoped with fear;
At night the glow-worm shone beneath the tree;
I led my Lucy to the spot, 'Look here,'
Oh! joy it was for her, and joy for me!

SIR WALTER SCOTT
1771-1832
An Hour With Thee!

An hour with thee! When earliest day
Dapples with gold the eastern grey,
Oh, what can frame my mind to bear
The toil and turmoil, cark and care,
New griefs, which coming hours unfold,
And sad remembrance of the old?
       One hour with thee.

One hour with thee! When burning June
Waves his red flag at pitch of noon;
What shall repay the faithful swain,
His labour on the sultry plain;
And, more than cave or sheltering bough,
Cool feverish blood and throbbing brow?
       One hour with thee.

One hour with thee! When sun is set,
Oh, what can teach me to forget
The thankless labours of the day;
The hopes, the wishes, flung away;
The increasing wants, and lessening gains,
The master's pride, who scorns my pains?
       One hour with thee.

Song

'A weary lot is thine, fair maid,
   A weary lot is thine!
To pull the thorn thy brow to braid,
   And press the rue for wine!
A lightsome eye, a soldier's mien,
   A feather of the blue,
A doublet of the Lincoln green,—
   No more of me you knew,
               My Love!
No more of me you knew.

This morn is merry June, I trow,
   The rose is budding fain;
But we shall bloom in winter snow,
   Ere we two meet again,'
He turned his charger as he spake,
   Upon the river shore,
He gave his bridle-reins a shake,
   Said, 'Adieu for evermore,
               My Love!
And adieu for evermore.'

WALTER SAVAGE LANDOR
1775–1864

Rose Aylmer

Ah, what avails the sceptred race!
　Ah, what the form divine!
What every virtue, every grace!
　Rose Aylmer, all were thine.

Rose Aylmer, whom these wakeful eyes
　May weep, but never see,
A night of memories and sighs
　I consecrate to thee.

Poem

You smiled, you spoke, and I believed,
By every word and smile deceived.
Another man would hope no more;
Nor hope I what I hoped before:
But let not this last wish be vain;
Deceive, deceive me once again!

THOMAS MOORE

1779–1852

Thee, Thee, Only Thee

The dawning of morn, the daylight's sinking,
The night's long hours still find me thinking
   Of thee, thee, only thee.
When friends are met, and goblets crown'd,
  And smiles are near that once enchanted,
Unreach'd by all that sunshine round,
  My soul, like some dark spot, is haunted
   By thee, thee, only thee.

Whatever in fame's high path could waken
My spirit once is now forsaken
   For thee, thee, only thee.
Like shores by which some headlong bark
  To the ocean hurries, resting never,
Life's scenes go by me, bright or dark
  I know not, heed not, hastening ever
   To thee, thee, only thee.

I have not a joy but of thy bringing,
And pain itself seems sweet when springing
   From thee, thee, only thee.
Like spells that nought on earth can break,
  Till lips that know the charm have spoken,
This heart, howe'er the world may wake
  Its grief, its scorn, can but be broken
   By thee, thee, only thee.

The Kiss

Give me, my love, that billing kiss
    I taught you one delicious night,
When, turning epicures in bliss,
    We tried inventions of delight.

Come, gently steal my lips along,
    And let your lips in murmurs move,–
Ah, no! – again – that kiss was wrong –
    How can you be so dull, my love?

'Cease, cease!' the blushing girl replied –
    And in her milky arms she caught me –
'How can you thus your pupil chide;
    You know *'twas in the dark* you taught me!'

Did Not

'Twas a new feeling – something more
Than we had dared to own before,
  Which then we hid not;
We saw it in each other's eye,
And wished, in every half-breathed sigh,
  To speak, but did not.

She felt my lips' impassioned touch –
'Twas the first time I dared so much,
  And yet she chid not;
But whispered o'er my burning brow,
'Oh, do you doubt I love you now?'
  Sweet soul! I did not.

Warmly I felt her bosom thrill,
I pressed it closer, closer still,
  Though gently bid not;
Till – oh! the world hath seldom heard
Of lovers, who so nearly erred,
  And yet, who did not.

GEORGE GORDON,
LORD BYRON
1788–1824

She Walks in Beauty

She walks in beauty, like the night
Of cloudless climes and starry skies,
And all that's best of dark and bright
Meets in her aspect and her eyes,
Thus mellow'd to that tender light
Which heaven to gaudy day denies.

One shade the more, one ray the less
Had half impair'd the nameless grace
Which waves in every raven tress
Or softly lightens o'er her face,
Where thoughts serenely sweet express
How pure, how dear their dwelling-place.

And on that cheek and o'er that brow
So soft, so calm, yet eloquent,
The smiles that win, the tints that glow
But tell of days in goodness spent,—
A mind at peace with all below,
A heart whose love is innocent.

Remember Thee!

Remember thee! remember thee!
   Till Lethe quench life's burning stream
Remorse and shame shall cling to thee,
   And haunt thee like a feverish dream!

Remember thee! Ay, doubt it not.
   Thy husband too shall think of thee!
By neither shalt thou be forgot,
   Thou *false* to him, thou *fiend* to me!

When We Two Parted

When we two parted
In silence and tears,
Half broken-hearted,
To sever for years,
Pale grew thy cheek and cold,
Colder thy kiss;
Truly that hour foretold
Sorrow to this!

The dew of the morning
Sunk chill on my brow;
It felt like the warning
Of what I feel now.
Thy vows are all broken,
And light is thy fame:
I hear thy name spoken
And share in its shame.

They name thee before me,
A knell to mine ear;
A shudder comes o'er me –
Why wert thou so dear?
They know not I knew thee
Who knew thee too well:
Long, long shall I rue thee
Too deeply to tell.

In secret we met:
In silence I grieve
That thy heart could forget,
Thy spirit deceive.
If I should meet thee
After long years,
How should I greet thee? –
With silence and tears.

PERCY BYSSHE SHELLEY

1792–1822

I Fear Thy Kisses

I fear thy kisses, gentle maiden;
Thou needest not fear mine;
My spirit is too deeply laden
Ever to burthen thine.

I fear thy mien, thy tones, thy motion;
Thou needest not fear mine;
Innocent is the heart's devotion
With which I worship thine.

Good-Night

Good-night? ah! no; the hour is ill
  Which severs those it should unite;
Let us remain together still,
  Then it will be good night.

How can I call the lone night good,
  Though thy sweet wishes wing its flight?
Be it not said, thought, understood,
  Then it will be good night.

To hearts which near each other move
  From evening close to morning light,
The night is good; because, my love
  They never say good-night.

Love's Philosophy

The fountains mingle with the river
  And the rivers with the Ocean,
The winds of Heaven mix for ever
  With a sweet emotion;
Nothing in the world is single;
  All things by a law divine
In one spirit meet and mingle.
  Why not I with thine? –

See the mountain kiss high Heaven
  And the waves clasp one another;
No sister-flower would be forgiven
  If it disdained its brother;
And the sunlight clasps the earth
  And the moonbeams kiss the sea:
What is all this sweet work worth
  If thou kiss not me?

To —

One word is too often profaned
  For me to profane it,
One feeling too falsely disdained
  For thee to disdain it;
One hope is too like despair
  For prudence to smother,
And pity from thee more dear
  Than that from another.

I can give not what men call love,
  But wilt thou accept not
The worship the heart lifts above
  And the Heavens reject not, –
The desire of the moth for the star,
  Of the night for the morrow,
The devotion to something afar
  From the sphere of our sorrow?

JOHN CLARE
1793–1869

I Hid My Love

I hid my love when young till I
Couldn't bear the buzzing of a fly;
I hid my love to my despite
Till I could not bear to look at light:
I dare not gaze upon her face
But left her memory in each place;
Where'er I saw a wild flower lie
I kissed and bade my love good-bye.

I met her in the greenest dells,
Where dewdrops pearl the wood bluebells;
The lost breeze kissed her bright blue eye,
The bee kissed and went singing by,
A sunbeam found a passage there,
A gold chain round her neck so fair;
As secret as the wild bee's song
She lay there all the summer long.

I hid my love in field and town
Till e'en the breeze would knock me down;
The bees seemed singing ballads o'er,
The fly's bass turned a lion's roar;
And even silence found a tongue,
To haunt me all the summer long;
The riddle nature could not prove
Was nothing else but secret love.

To Mary

I sleep with thee, and wake with thee,
 And yet thou art not there;
I fill my arms with thoughts of thee,
 And press the common air.
Thy eyes are gazing upon mine,
 When thou art out of sight;
My lips are always touching thine,
 At morning, noon, and night.

I think and speak of other things
 To keep my mind at rest:
But still to thee my memory clings
 Like love in woman's breast.
I hide it from the world's wide eye,
 And think and speak contrary;
But soft the wind comes from the sky,
 And whispers tales of Mary.

The night wind whispers in my ear,
 The moon shines in my face;
A burden still of chilling fear
 I find in every place.
The breeze is whispering in the bush,
 And the dews fall from the tree,
All sighing on, and will not hush,
 Some pleasant tales of thee.

With Garments Flowing

Come, come, my love, the bush is growing.
  The linnet sings the tune again
He sung when thou with garmemts flowing
  Went talking with me down the lane.
Dreaming of beauty ere I found thee,
  And musing by the bushes green;
The wind, enamoured, streaming round thee
  Painted the visions I had seen.

I guessed thy face without the knowing
  Was beautiful as e'er was seen;
I thought so by the garments flowing
  And gait as airy as a queen;
Thy shape, thy size, could not deceive me:
  Beauty seemed hid in every limb;
And then thy face, when seen, believe me,
  Made every former fancy dim.

Yes, when thy face in beauty brightened
  The music of a voice divine,
Upon my heart thy sweetness lightened;
  Life, love, that moment, all were thine;
All I imagined musing lonely,
  When dreaming 'neath the greenwood tree,
Seeming to fancy visions only,
  Breathed living when I met with thee.

I wander oft, not to forget thee
  But just to feel those joys again.
When by the hawbush stile I met thee
  And heard thy voice adown the lane
Return me its good-humoured greeting:
  And oh, what music met my ear!
And then thy looks of wonder meeting,
  To see me come and talk so near!

Thy face that held no sort of scorning,
   Thy careless jump to reach the may;
That bush—I saw it many a morning
   And hoped to meet thee many a day;
Till winter came and stripped the bushes,
   The thistle withered on the moors,
Hopes sighed like winds along the rushes—
   I could not meet thee out of doors.

But winter's gone and spring is going
   And by thy own fireside I've been,
And told thee, dear, with garments flowing
   I met thee when the spring was green;
When travellers through snow-deserts rustle,
   Far from the strife of humankind,
How little seems the noise and bustle
   Of places they have left behind!

And on that long-remembered morning
   When first I lost this heart of mine,
Fame, all I'd hoped for, turned to scorning
   And love and hope lived wholly thine;
I told thee, and with rapture glowing
   I heard thee more than once declare,
That down the lane with garments flowing
   Thou with the spring wouldst wander there.

First Love

I ne'er was struck before that hour
  With love so sudden and so sweet,
Her face it bloomed like a sweet flower
  And stole my heart away complete.
My face turned pale as deadly pale,
  My legs refused to walk away,
And when she looked, what could I ail?
  My life and all seemed turned to clay.

And then my blood rushed to my face
  And took my eyesight quite away,
The trees and bushes round the place
  Seemed midnight at noonday.
I could not see a single thing,
  Words from my eyes did start –
They spoke as chords do from the string,
  And blood burnt round my heart.

Are flowers the winter's choice?
  Is love's bed always snow?
She seemed to hear my silent voice,
  Not love's appeals to know.
I never saw so sweet a face
  As that I stood before.
My heart has left its dwelling-place
  And can return no more.

Mary

It is the evening hour,
    How silent all doth lie:
The horned moon she shows her face
    In the river with the sky.
Prest by the path on which we pass,
The flaggy lake lies still as glass.

Spirit of her I love,
    Whispering to me
Stores of sweet visions as I rove,
    Here stop, and crop with me
Sweet flowers that in the still hour grew –
We'll take them home, nor shake off the bright dew.

Mary, or sweet spirit of thee,
    As the bright sun shines to-morrow
Thy dark eyes these flowers shall see,
    Gathered by me in sorrow,
In the still hour when my mind was free
To walk alone – yet wish I walked with thee.

JOHN KEATS
1795–1821

Sonnet

Bright star! would I were steadfast as thou art—
  Not in lone splendour hung aloft the night
And watching, with eternal lids apart,
  Like nature's patient, sleepless Eremite,
The moving waters at their priestlike task
  Of pure ablution round earth's human shores,
Or gazing on the new soft fallen mask
  Of snow upon the mountains and the moors—
No—yet still steadfast, still unchangeable,
  Pillow'd upon my fair love's ripening breast,
To feel for ever its soft fall and swell,
  Awake for ever in a sweet unrest,
Still, still to hear her tender-taken breath,
And so live ever—or else swoon to death.

Song

O blush not so! O blush not so!
  Or I shall think you knowing;
And if you smile the blushing while,
  Then maidenheads are going.

There's a blush for won't, and a blush for shan't,
  And a blush for having done it:
There's a blush for thought, and a blush for naught,
  And a blush for just begun it.

O sigh not so! O sigh not so!
  For it sounds of Eve's sweet pippin;
By those loosened lips you have tasted the pips
  And fought in an amorous nipping.

Will you play once more at nice-cut-core,
  For it only will last our youth out?
And we have the prime of the kissing time,
  We have not one sweet tooth out.

There's a sigh for yes, and a sigh for no,
  And a sigh for I can't bear it!
O what can be done, shall we stay or run?
  O, cut the sweet apple and share it!

Where Be You Going, You Devon Maid?

Where be you going, you Devon maid?
   And what have ye there in the basket?
Ye tight little fairy, just fresh from the dairy,
   Will ye give me some cream if I ask it?

I love your hills and I love your dales,
   And I love your flocks a-bleating;
But oh, on the heather to lie together,
   With both our hearts a-beating!

I'll put your basket all safe in a nook;
   Your shawl I'll hang on a willow;
And we will sigh in the daisy's eye,
   And kiss on a grass-green pillow.

THOMAS HOOD

1799–1845

Ruth

She stood breast high amid the corn,
Clasped by the golden light of morn,
Like the sweetheart of the sun,
Who many a glowing kiss had won.

On her cheek an autumn flush,
Deeply ripened; – such a blush
In the midst of brown was born,
Like red poppies grown with corn.

Round her eyes her tresses fell,
Which were blackest none could tell,
But long lashes veiled a light,
That had else been all too bright.

And her hat, with shady brim,
Made her tressy forehead dim; –
Thus she stood amid the stooks,
Praising God with sweetest looks: –

Sure, I said, heaven did not mean,
Where I reap thou shouldst but glean,
Lay thy sheaf adown and come,
Share my harvest and my home.

ELIZABETH BARRETT BROWNING
1806–1861

Sonnet 43 from Sonnets from the Portuguese

How do I love thee? Let me count the ways.
I love thee to the depth and breadth and height
My soul can reach, when feeling out of sight
For the ends of Being and ideal Grace.
I love thee to the level of everyday's
Most quiet need, by sun and candle-light.
I love thee freely, as men strive for Right;
I love thee purely, as they turn from Praise.
I love thee with the passion put to use
In my old griefs, and with my childhood's faith.
I love thee with a love I seemed to lose
With my lost saints,—I love thee with the breath,
Smiles, tears, of all my life!—and, if God choose,
I shall but love thee better after death.

Sonnet 44 from Sonnets from the Portuguese

Belovèd, thou has brought me many flowers
Plucked in the garden, all the summer through
And winter, and it seemed as if they grew
In this close room, nor missed the sun and showers.
So, in the like name of that love of ours,
Take back these thoughts which here unfolded too,
And which on warm and cold days I withdrew
From my heart's ground. Indeed, those beds and bowers
Be overgrown with bitter weeds and rue,
And wait thy weeding; yet here's eglantine,
Here's ivy! – take them, as I used to do
Thy flowers, and keep them where they shall not pine.
Instruct thine eyes to keep their colours true,
And tell thy soul their roots are left in mine.

EDGAR ALLAN POE

1809–1849

To Helen

Helen, thy beauty is to me
  Like those Nicean barks of yore,
That gently, o'er a perfumed sea,
  The weary, wayworn wanderer bore
  To his own native shore.

On desperate seas long wont to roam,
  Thy hyacinth hair, thy classic face,
Thy Naiad airs have brought me home
  To the glory that was Greece,
  To the grandeur that was Rome.

Lo! in yon brilliant window niche,
  How statue-like I see thee stand,
  The agate lamp within thy hand!
Ah, Psyche, from the regions which
  Are Holy Land!

A Dream Within A Dream

Take this kiss upon the brow!
And, in parting from you now,
Thus much let me avow—
You are not wrong, who deem
That my days have been a dream:
Yet if hope has flown away
In a night, or in a day,
In a vision, or in none,
Is it therefore the less *gone*?
All that we see or seem
Is but a dream within a dream.

I stand amid the roar
Of a surf-tormented shore,
And I hold within my hand
Grains of the golden sand—
How few! yet how they creep
Through my fingers to the deep,
While I weep—while I weep!
O God! can I not grasp
Them with a tighter clasp?
O God! can I not save
One from the pitiless wave?
Is *all* that we see or seem
But a dream within a dream?

To One In Paradise

Thou wast that all to me, love,
  For which my soul did pine –
A green isle in the sea, love,
  A fountain and a shrine,
All wreathed with fairy fruits and flowers,
  And all the flowers were mine.

Ah, dream too bright to last!
  Ah, starry Hope! that didst arise
But to be overcast!
  A voice from out the Future cries,
'On! on!' – but o'er the Past
  (Dim gulf!) my spirit hovering lies
Mute, motionless, aghast!

For, alas! alas! with me
  The light of Life is o'er!
No more – no more – no more –
(Such language holds the solemn sea
  To the sands upon the shore)
Shall bloom the thunder-blasted tree,
  Or the stricken eagle soar!

And all my days are trances,
  And all my nightly dreams
Are where thy grey eye glances,
  And where thy footstep gleams –
In what ethereal dances,
  By what eternal streams.

ALFRED, LORD TENNYSON
1809–1892

Poem

Oh! that 'twere possible,
    After long grief and pain,
To find the arms of my true-love
    Round me once again!

When I was wont to meet her
   In the silent woody places
    Of the land that gave me birth,
  We stood tranced in long embraces,
Mixed with kisses sweeter, sweeter,
    Than any thing on earth.

A shadow flits before me –
    Not thou, but like to thee.
Ah God! that it were possible
    For one short hour to see
The souls we loved, that they might tell us
    What and where they be.

It leads me forth at evening,
    It lightly winds and steals
In a cold white robe before me,
    When all my spirit reels
At the shouts, the leagues of lights,
    And the roaring of the wheels.

Half the night I waste in sighs,
    In a wakeful doze I sorrow
For the hand, the lips, the eyes –
    For the meeting of tomorrow,
      The delight of happy laughter,
The delight of low replies.

The Daisy

O love, what hours were thine and mine,
In lands of palm and southern pine;
    In lands of palm, of orange-blossom,
Of olive, aloe, and maize and vine.

Nor knew we well what pleased us most,
Not the clipt palm of which they boast;
    But distant colour, happy hamlet,
A moulder'd citadel on the coast,

Or tower, or high hill-convent, seen
A light amid its olives green;
    Or olive-hoary cape in ocean;
Or rosy blossom in hot ravine.

What more? we took our last adieu,
And up the snowy Splugen drew,
    But ere we reach'd the highest summit
I pluck'd a daisy, I gave it you.

It told of England then to me,
And now it tells of Italy.
    O love, we two shall go no longer
To lands of summer across the sea;

So dear a life your arms enfold
Whose crying is a cry for gold:
    Yet here to-night in this dark city,
When ill and weary, alone and cold,

I found, tho' crush'd to hard and dry,
This nursling of another sky
    Still in the little book you lent me,
And where you tenderly laid it by:

And I forgot the clouded Forth,
The gloom that saddens Heaven and Earth
   The bitter east, the misty summer
And gray metropolis of the North.

Perchance, to lull the throbs of pain,
Perchance, to charm a vacant brain,
   Perchance, to dream you still beside me,
My fancy fled to the South again.

Ask Me No More

Ask me no more: the moon may draw the sea;
  The cloud may stoop from heaven and take the shape
  With fold to fold, of mountain or of cape;
But O too fond, when have I answer'd thee?
                                    Ask me no more.

Ask me no more: what answer should I give?
  I love not hollow cheek or faded eye:
  Yet, O my friend, I will not have thee die!
Ask me no more, lest I should bid thee live;
                                    Ask me no more.

Ask me no more: thy fate and mine are seal'd,
  I strove against the stream and all in vain;
  Let the great river take me to the main:
No more, dear love, for at a touch I yield;
                                    Ask me no more.

Now Sleeps the Crimson Petal

Now sleeps the crimson petal, now the white;
Nor waves the cypress in the palace walk;
Nor winks the gold fin in the porphyry font.
The fire-fly wakens; waken thou with me.

Now droops the milk-white peacock like a ghost,
And like a ghost she glimmers on to me.

Now lies the Earth all Danaë to the stars,
And all thy heart lies open unto me.

Now slides the silent meteor on, and leaves
A shining furrow, as thy thoughts in me.

Now folds the lily all her sweetness up,
And slips into the bosom of the lake:
So fold thyself, my dearest, thou, and slip
Into my bosom and be lost in me.

Fatima

O Love, Love, Love! O withering might!
O sun, that from thy noonday height
Shudderest when I strain my sight,
Throbbing thro' all thy heat and light,
   Lo, falling from my constant mind,
   Lo, parch'd and wither'd, deaf and blind,
   I whirl like leaves in roaring wind.

Last night I wasted hateful hours
Below thy city's eastern towers:
I thirsted for the brooks, the showers:
I roll'd among the tender flowers:
   I crush'd them on my breast, my mouth;
   I look'd athwart the burning drouth
   Of that long desert to the south.

Last night, when some one spoke his name,
From my swift blood that went and came
A thousand little shafts of flame
Were shiver'd in my narrow frame.
   O Love, O fire! once he drew
   With one long kiss my whole soul thro'
   My lips, as sunlight drinketh dew.

Before he mounts the hill, I know
He cometh quickly: from below
Sweet gales, as from deep gardens, blow
Before him, striking on my brow.
   In my dry brain my spirit soon,
   Down-deepening from swoon to swoon,
   Faints like a dazzled morning moon.

The wind sounds like a silver wire,
And from beyond the noon a fire
Is pour'd upon the hills, and nigher
The skies stoop down in their desire;
   And, isled in sudden seas of light,
   My heart, pierced thro' with fierce delight,
   Bursts into blossom in his sight.

My whole soul waiting silently,
All naked in a sultry sky,
Droops blinded with his shining eye:
I *will* possess him or will die.
   I will grow round him in his place,
   Grow, live, die looking on his face,
   Die, dying clasp'd in his embrace.

Marriage Morning

Light, so low upon earth,
   You send a flash to the sun.
Here is the golden close of love,
   All my wooing is done.
Oh, the woods and the meadows,
   Woods where we hid from the wet,
Stiles where we stay'd to be kind,
   Meadows in which we met!

Light, so low in the vale
   You flash and lighten afar,
For this is the golden morning of love,
   And you are his morning star.
Flash, I am coming, I come,
   By meadow and stile and wood,
Oh, lighten into my eyes and heart,
   Into my heart and my blood!

Heart, are you great enough
   For a love that never tires?
O heart, are you great enough for love?
   I have heard of thorns and briers.
Over the thorns and briers,
   Over the meadows and stiles,
Over the world to the end of it
   Flash for a million miles.

ROBERT BROWNING

1812–1889

The Lost Mistress

All's over, then: does truth sound bitter
  As one at first believes?
Hark, 'tis the sparrows' good-night twitter
  About your cottage eaves!

And the leaf-buds on the vine are woolly,
  I noticed that, today;
One day more bursts them open fully
  – You know the red turns grey.

Tomorrow we meet the same then, dearest?
  May I take your hand in mine?
Mere friends are we, – well, friends the merest
  Keep much that I resign:

For each glance of the eye so bright and black,
  Though I keep with heart's endeavour, –
Your voice, when you wish the snowdrops back,
  Though it stay in my soul for ever! –

Yet I will but say what mere friends say,
  Or only a thought stronger;
I will hold your hand but as long as all may,
  Or so very little longer!

Respectability

Dear, had the world in its caprice
   Deigned to proclaim 'I know you both,
Have recognized your plighted troth
   Am sponsor for you: live in peace!'—
How many precious months and years
   Of youth had passed, that speed so fast,
Before we found it out at last,
   The world, and what it fears?

How much of priceless life were spent
   With men that every virtue decks,
And women models of their sex
   Society's true ornament,—
Ere we dared wander, nights like this,
   Through wind and rain, and watch the Seine,
And feel the Boulevard break again
   To warmth and light and bliss?

I know! the world proscribes not love;
   Allows my finger to caress
Your lip's contour and downiness,
   Provided it supply a glove.
The world's good word!—the Institute!
   Guizot receives Montalembert!
Eh? Down the court three lampions flare:
   Put forward your best foot!

Never the Time and the Place

Never the time and the place
　　And the loved one all together!
This path – how soft to pace!
　　This May – what magic weather!
Where is the loved one's face?
In a dream that loved one's face meets mine,
　　But the house is narrow, the place is bleak
Where, outside, rain and wind combine
　　With a furtive ear, if I strive to speak,
　　With hostile eye at my flushing cheek,
With a malice that marks each word, each sign!
O enemy sly and serpentine
　　Uncoil thee from the waking man!
　　　　Do I hold the Past
　　　　Thus firm and fast
　　　Yet doubt if the Future hold I can
This path so soft to pace shall lead,
Thro' the magic of May to herself indeed!
Or narrow if needs the house must be,
Outside are the storms and strangers: we –
Oh, close, safe, warm sleep I and she,
– I and she!

Meeting At Night

I

The grey sea and the long black land;
And the yellow half-moon large and low;
And the startled little waves that leap
In fiery ringlets from their sleep,
As I gain the cove with pushing prow,
And quench its speed i' the slushy sand.

II

Then a mile of warm sea-scented beach;
Three fields to cross till a farm appears;
A tap at the pane, the quick sharp scratch
And blue spurt of a lighted match,
And a voice less loud, thro' its joys and fears,
Than the two hearts beating each to each!

EMILY BRONTË

1818–1848

Remembrance

Cold in the earth, and the deep snow piled above thee!
Far, far removed, cold in the dreary grave!
Have I forgot, my Only Love, to love thee,
Severed at last by Time's all-wearing wave?

Now, when alone, do my thoughts no longer hover
Over the mountains on Angora's shore;
Resting their wings where heath and fern-leaves cover
That noble heart for ever, ever more?

Cold in the earth, and fifteen wild Decembers
From those brown hills have melted into spring –
Faithful indeed is the spirit that remembers
After such years of change and suffering!

Sweet Love of youth, forgive if I forget thee
While the World's tide is bearing me along:
Sterner desires and darker hopes beset me,
Hopes which obscure but cannot do thee wrong.

No other Sun has lightened up my heaven;
No other Star has ever shone for me:
All my life's bliss from thy dear life was given –
All my life's bliss is in the grave with thee.

But when the days of golden dreams had perished
And even Despair was powerless to destroy,
Then did I learn how existence could be cherished,
Strengthened and fed without the aid of joy;

Then did I check the tears of useless passion,
Weaned my young soul from yearning after thine;
Sternly denied its burning wish to hasten
Down to that tomb already more than mine!

And even yet, I dare not let it languish,
Dare not indulge in Memory's rapturous pain;
Once drinking deep of that divinest anguish,
How could I seek the empty world again?

MATTHEW ARNOLD

1822–1888

Isolation. To Marguerite

We were apart; yet, day by day,
I bade my heart more constant be.
I bade it keep the world away,
And grow a home for only thee;
Nor feared but thy love likewise grew,
Like mine, each day, more tried, more true.

The fault was grave! I might have known,
What far too soon, alas! I learned –
The heart can bind itself alone,
And faith may oft be unreturned.
Self-swayed our feelings ebb and swell –
Thou lov'st no more; – Farewell! Farewell!

Farewell! – and thou, thou lonely heart,
Which never yet without remorse
Even for a moment didst depart
From thy remote and spherèd course
To haunt the place where passions reign –
Back to thy solitude again!

Back! with the conscious thrill of shame
Which Luna felt, that summer-night,
Flash through her pure immortal frame,
When she forsook the starry height
To hang over Endymion's sleep
Upon the pine-grown Latmian steep.

Yet she, chaste queen, had never proved
How vain a thing is mortal love,
Wandering in Heaven, far removed.
But thou hast long had place to prove
This truth – to prove, and make thine own:
'Thou has been, shalt be, art, alone.'

Or, if not quite alone, yet they
Which touch thee are unmating things –
Ocean and clouds and night and day;
Lorn autumns and triumphant springs;
And life, and others' joy and pain,
And love, if love, of happier men.

COVENTRY PATMORE
1823–1896

A Farewell

With all my will, but much against my heart,
We two now part.
My Very Dear,
Our solace is, the sad road lies so clear.
It needs no art,
With faint, averted feet
And many a tear,
In our opposed paths to persevere.
Go thou to East, I West.
We will not say
There's any hope, it is so far away.
But, O, my Best,
When the one darling of our widowhead,
The nursling Grief,
Is dead,
And no dews blur our eyes
To see the peach-bloom come in evening skies,
Perchance we may,
Where now this night is day,
And even through faith of still averted feet,
Making full circle of our banishment,
Amazed meet;
The bitter journey to the bourne so sweet
Seasoning the termless feast of our content
With tears of recognition never dry.

WILLIAM ALLINGHAM

1824–1889

Song

I walk'd in the lonesome evening,
  And who so sad as I,
When I saw the young men and maidens
  Merrily passing by.
    To thee, my Love, to thee—
    So fain would I come to thee!
While the ripples fold upon sands of gold
  And I look across the sea.

I stretch out my hands; who will clasp them?
  I call,—thou repliest no word:
O why should heart-longing be weaker
  Than the waving wings of a bird!
    To thee, my Love, to thee—
    So fain would I come to thee!
For the tide's at rest from east to west,
  And I look across the sea.

There's joy in the hopeful morning,
  There's peace in the parting day,
There's sorrow with every lover
  Whose true love is far away.
    To thee, my Love, to thee—
    So fain would I come to thee!
And the water's bright in a still moonlight,
  As I look across the sea.

DANTE GABRIEL ROSSETTI

1828–1882

Poem

Your hands lie open in the long fresh grass,
 The finger-points look through like rosy blooms;
Your eyes smile peace. The pasture gleams and glooms
 'Neath billowing skies that scatter and amass.
All round our nest, far as the eye can pass,
 Are golden kingcup-fields with silver edge
Where the cow-parsley skirts the hawthorn-hedge.
 'Tis visible silence, still as the hour-glass.

Deep in the sun-searched growths the dragon-fly
 Hangs like a blue thread loosened from the sky:
So this winged hour is dropt to us from above.
 Oh! clasp we to our hearts, for deathless dower,
This close-companioned inarticulate hour
 When twofold silence was the song of love.

An Old Song Ended

'How should I your true love know
     From another one?'
'By his cockle-hat and staff
     And his sandal-shoon.'

'And what signs have told you now
     That he hastens home?'
'Lo! the spring is nearly gone,
     He is nearly come.'

'For a token is there nought,
     Say, that he should bring?'
'He will bear a ring I gave
     And another ring.'

'How may I, when he shall ask,
     Tell him who lies there?'
'Nay, but leave my face unveiled
     And unbound my hair.'

'Can you say to me some word
     I shall say to him?'
'Say I'm looking in his eyes
     Though my eyes are dim.'

Sudden Light

I have been here before,
  But when or how I cannot tell:
I know the grass beyond the door,
  The sweet keen smell,
The sighing sound, the lights around the shore.

You have been mine before,–
  How long ago I may not know:
But just when at that swallow's soar
  Your neck turned so,
Some veil did fall, – I knew it all of yore.

Has this been thus before?
  And shall not thus time's eddying flight
Still with our lives our love restore
  In death's despite,
And day and night yield one delight once more?

EMILY DICKINSON
1830–1886

Parting

My life closed twice before its close –
It yet remains to see
If Immortality unveil
A third event to me

So huge, so hopeless to conceive
As these that twice befell.
Parting is all we know of heaven,
And all we need of hell.

CHRISTINA ROSSETTI
1830–1894

Song

When I am dead, my dearest,
Sing no sad songs for me;
Plant thou no roses at my head,
Nor shady cypress tree:
Be the green grass above me
With showers and dewdrops wet;
And if thou wilt, remember,
And if thou wilt, forget.

I shall not see the shadows,
I shall not feel the rain;
I shall not hear the nightingale
Sing on, as if in pain;
And dreaming through the twilight
That doth not rise nor set,
Haply I may remember,
And haply may forget.

The First Day

I wish I could remember the first day,
First hour, first moment of your meeting me;
If bright or dim the season, it might be
Summer or winter for aught I can say.
So unrecorded did it slip away,
So blind was I to see and to foresee,
So dull to mark the budding of my tree
That would not blossom yet for many a May.

If only I could recollect it! Such
A day of days! I let it come and go
As traceless as a thaw of bygone snow.
It seemed to mean so little, meant so much!
If only now I could recall that touch,
First touch of hand in hand! – Did one but know!

Remember

Remember me when I am gone away,
Gone far away into the silent land;
When you can no more hold me by the hand,
Nor I half turn to go yet turning stay.
Remember me when no more day by day
You tell me of our future that you plann'd:
Only remember me; you understand
It will be late to counsel then or pray.
Yet if you should forget me for a while
And afterwards remember, do not grieve:
For if the darkness and corruption leave
A vestige of the thoughts that once I had,
Better by far you should forget and smile
Than that you should remember and be sad.

ALGERNON CHARLES SWINBURNE
1837–1909

In the Orchard

Leave go my hands, let me catch breath and see;
Let the dew-fall drench either side of me;
   Clear apple-leaves are soft upon that moon
Seen sidelong like a blossom in the tree;
   And God, ah God, that day should be so soon.

The grass is thick and cool, it lets us lie.
Kissed upon either cheek and either eye,
   I turn to thee as some green afternoon
Turns toward sunset, and is loth to die;
   Ah God, ah God, that day should be so soon.

Lie closer, lean your face upon my side,
Feel where the dew fell that has hardly dried,
   Hear how the blood beats that went nigh to swoon;
The pleasure lives there when the sense has died,
   Ah God, ah God, that day should be so soon.

O my fair lord, I charge you leave me this:
Is it not sweeter than a foolish kiss?
   Nay take it then, my flower, my first in June,
My rose, so like a tender mouth it is:
   Ah God, ah God, that day should be so soon.

Love, till dawn sunder night from day with fire
Dividing my delight and my desire,
   The crescent life and love the plenilune,
Love me though dusk begin and dark retire;
   Ah God, ah God, that day should be so soon.

Ah, my heart fails, my blood draws back; I know,
When life runs over, life is near to go;
   And with the slain of love love's ways are strewn,
And with their blood, if love will have it so;
   Ah God, ah God, that day should be so soon.

Ah, do thy will now; slay me if thou wilt;
There is no building now the walls are built,
   No quarrying now the corner-stone is hewn,
No drinking now the vine's whole blood is spilt;
   Ah God, ah God, that day should be so soon.

Nay, slay me now; nay, for I will be slain;
Pluck thy red pleasure from the teeth of pain,
   Break down thy vine ere yet grape-gatherers prune,
Slay me ere day can slay desire again;
   Ah God, ah God, that day should be so soon.

Yea, with thy sweet lips, with thy sweet sword; yea
Take life and all, for I will die, I say;
   Love, I gave love, is life a better boon?
For sweet night's sake I will not live till day;
   Ah God, ah God, that day should be so soon.

Nay, I will sleep then only; nay, but go.
Ah sweet, too sweet to me, my sweet, I know
   Love, sleep, and death go to the sweet same tune;
Hold my hair fast, and kiss me through it soon.
   Ah God, ah God, that day should be so soon.

Love and Sleep

Lying asleep between the strokes of night
  I saw my love lean over my sad bed,
  Pale as the duskiest lily's leaf or head,
Smooth-skinned and dark, with bare throat made to bite,
Too wan for blushing and too warm for white,
  But perfect-coloured without white or red.
And her lips opened amorously, and said –
I wist not what, saving one word – Delight.

And all her face was honey to my mouth,
  And all her body pasture to mine eyes;
    The long lithe arms and hotter hands than fire,
The quivering flanks, hair smelling of the south,
  The bright light feet, the splendid supple thighs
    And glittering eyelids of my soul's desire.

169

WILFRID BLUNT

1840-1922

Farewell To Juliet

I see you, Juliet, still, with your straw hat
Loaded with vines, and with your dear pale face,
On which those thirty years so lightly sat,
And the white outline of your muslin dress.
You wore a little *fichu* trimmed with lace
And crossed in front, as was the fashion then,
Bound at your waist with a broad band or sash,
All white and fresh and virginally plain.
There was a sound of shouting far away
Down in the valley, as they called to us,
And you, with hands clasped seeming still to pray
Patience of fate, stood listening to me thus
With heaving bosom. There a rose lay curled.
It was the reddest rose in all the world.

THOMAS HARDY

1840–1928

Faintheart in a Railway Train

At nine in the morning there passed a church,
At ten there passed me by the sea,
At twelve a town of smoke and smirch,
At two a forest of oak and birch,
   And then, on a platform, she:

A radiant stranger, who saw not me.
I said, 'Get out to her do I dare?'
But I kept my seat in my search for a plea,
And the wheels moved on. O could it but be
   That I had alighted there!

After a Journey

Hereto I come to view a voiceless ghost;
　　Whither, O whither will its whim now draw me?
Up the cliff, down, till I'm lonely, lost,
　　And the unseen waters' ejaculations awe me.
Where you will next be there's no knowing,
　　Facing round about me everywhere,
　　　　With your nut-coloured hair,
And gray eyes, and rose-flush coming and going.

Yes: I have re-entered your olden haunts at last;
　　Through the years, through the dead scenes I have tracked
　　　　you;
What have you now found to say of our past—
　　Scanned across the dark space wherein I have lacked you?
Summer gave us sweets, but autumn wrought division?
　　Things were not lastly as firstly well
　　　　With us twain, you tell?
But all's closed now, despite Time's derision.

I see what you are doing: you are leading me on
　　To the spots we knew when we haunted here together,
The waterfall, above which the mist-bow shone
　　At the then fair hour in the then fair weather,
And the cave just under, with a voice still so hollow
　　That it seems to call out to me from forty years ago,
　　　　When you were all aglow,
And not the thin ghost that I now fraily follow!

Ignorant of what there is flitting here to see,
　　The waked birds preen and the seals flop lazily,
Soon you will have, Dear, to vanish from me,
　　For the stars close their shutters and the dawn whitens
　　　　hazily.

Trust me, I mind not, though Life lours,
    The bringing me here; nay, bring me here again!
        I am just the same as when
Our days were a joy, and our paths through flowers.

The Voice

Woman much missed, how you call to me, call to me,
Saying that now you are not as you were
When you had changed from the one who was all to me,
But as at first, when our day was fair.

Can it be you that I hear? Let me view you, then,
Standing as when I drew near to the town
Where you would wait for me: yes, as I knew you then,
Even to the original air-blue gown!

Or is it only the breeze, in its listlessness
Travelling across the wet mead to me here,
You being ever consigned to existlessness,
Heard no more again far or near?

    Thus I: faltering forward,
    Leaves around me falling,
Wind oozing thin through the thorn from norward,
    And the woman calling.

I Said To Love

I said to Love,
'It is not now as in old days
When men adored thee and thy ways
    All else above;
Named thee the Boy, the Bright, the One
Who spread a heaven beneath the sun,'
    I said to Love.

I said to Love,
'We now know more of thee than then;
We were but weak in judgment when,
    With hearts abrim,
We clamoured thee that thou would'st please
Inflict on us thine agonies,'
    I said to him.

I said to him,
'Thou art not young, thou art not fair,
No elfin darts, no cherub air,
    Nor swan, nor dove
Are thine; but features pitiless,
And iron daggers of distress,'
    I said to Love.

    'Depart then, Love! ...
—Man's race shall perish, threatenest thou,
Without thy kindling coupling-vow?
The age to come the men of now
    Know nothing of—
We fear not such a threat from thee;
We are too old in apathy!
Mankind shall cease.—So let it be,'
    I said to Love.

THOMAS HARDY

A Broken Appointment

You did not come,
And marching Time drew on, and wore me numb.–
Yet less for loss of your dear presence there
Than that I thus found lacking in your make
That high compassion which can overbear
Reluctance for pure lovingkindness' sake
Grieved I, when, as the hope-hour stroked its sum
               You did not come.

You love not me,
And love alone can lend you loyalty;
–I know and knew it. But, unto the store
Of human deeds divine in all but name,
Was it not worth a little hour or more
To add yet this: Once you, a woman, came
To soothe a time-torn man; even though it be
               You love not me?

A Thunderstorm In Town

She wore a new 'terra-cotta' dress,
And we stayed, because of the pelting storm,
Within the hansom's dry recess,
Though the horse had stopped; yea, motionless
  We sat on, snug and warm.

Then the downpour ceased, to my sharp sad pain
And the glass that had screened our forms before
Flew up, and out she sprang to her door:
I should have kissed her if the rain
  Had lasted a minute more.

176

ROBERT BRIDGES
1844-1930

I Will Not Let Thee Go

I will not let thee go.
Ends all our month-long love in this?
    Can it be summed up so,
    Quit in a single kiss?
I will not let thee go.

I will not let thee go.
If thy words' breath could scare thy deeds,
    As the soft south can blow
    And toss the feathered seeds,
Then might I let thee go.

I will not let thee go.
Had not the great sun seen, I might;
    Or were he reckoned slow
    To bring the false to light,
Then might I let thee go.

I will not let thee go.
The stars that crowd the summer skies
    Have watched us so below
    With all their million eyes,
I dare not let thee go.

I will not let thee go.
Have we not chid the changeful moon,
    Now rising late and now
    Because she set too soon,
And shall I let thee go?

I will not let thee go.
Have not the young flowers been content,
   Plucked ere their buds could blow,
   To seal our sacrament?
   I cannot let thee go.

   I will not let thee go.
I hold thee by too many bands:
   Thou sayest farewell, and lo!
   I have thee by the hands,
   And will not let thee go.

FRANCIS WILLIAM BOURDILLON

1852–1921

Night

The night has a thousand eyes,
   And the day but one;
Yet the light of the bright world dies
   With the dying sun.

The mind has a thousand eyes,
   And the heart but one;
Yet the light of a whole life dies,
   When love is done.

A. E. HOUSMAN
1859–1936

Because I Liked You Better

Because I liked you better
  Than suits a man to say,
It irked you, and I promised
  To throw the thought away.

To put the world between us
  We parted, stiff and dry;
'Good-bye', said you, 'forget me.'
  'I will, no fear', said I.

If here, where clover whitens
  The dead man's knoll, you pass,
And no tall flower to meet you
  Starts in the trefoiled grass,

Halt by the headstone naming
  The heart no longer stirred,
And say the lad that loved you
  Was one that kept his word.

W. B. YEATS
1865–1939

When You are Old

When you are old and grey and full of sleep,
And nodding by the fire, take down this book,
And slowly read, and dream of the soft look
Your eyes had once, and of their shadows deep;

How many loved your moments of glad grace,
And loved your beauty with love false or true,
But one man loved the pilgrim soul in you,
And loved the sorrows of your changing face;

And bending down beside the glowing bars,
Murmur, a little sadly, how Love fled
And paced upon the mountains overhead
And his his face amid a crowd of stars.

117 The Ragged Wood

O hurry where by water among the trees
The delicate-stepping stag and his lady sigh,
When they have but looked upon their images–
Would none had ever loved but you and I!

Or have you heard that sliding silver-shoed
Pale silver-proud queen-woman of the sky,
When the sun looked out of his golden hood?–
O that none ever loved but you and I!

O hurry to the ragged wood, for there
I will drive all those lovers out and cry–
O my share of the world, O yellow hair!
No one has ever loved but you and I.

Brown Penny

I whispered, 'I am too young,'
And then, 'I am old enough';
Wherefore I threw a penny
To find out if I might love.
'Go and love, go and love, young man,
If the lady be young and fair.'
Ah, penny, brown penny, brown penny,
I am looped in the loops of her hair.

O love is the crooked thing,
There is nobody wise enough
To find out all that is in it,
For he would be thinking of love
Till the stars had run away
And the shadows eaten the moon.
Ah, penny, brown penny, brown penny,
One cannot begin it too soon.

ERNEST DOWSON

1867–1900

Non Sum Qualis Eram Bonae Sub Regno Cynarae

Last night, ah, yesternight, betwixt her lips and mine
There fell thy shadow, Cynara! thy breath was shed
Upon my soul between the kisses and the wine;
And I was desolate and sick of an old passion,
　　Yea, I was desolate and bowed my head:
I have been faithful to thee, Cynara! in my fashion.

I have forgot much, Cynara! gone with the wind,
Flung roses, roses riotously with the throng,
Dancing, to put thy pale, lost lilies out of mind;
But I was desolate and sick of an old passion,
　　Yea, all the time, because the dance was long:
I have been faithful to thee, Cynara! in my fashion.

I cried for madder music and for stronger wine,
But when the feast is finished and lamps expire,
Then falls thy shadow, Cynara! the night is thine;
And I am desolate and sick of an old passion,
　　Yea, hungry for the lips of my desire:
I have been faithful to thee, Cynara! in my fashion.

HILAIRE BELLOC
1870–1953

Juliet

How did the party go in Portman Square?
I cannot tell you; Juliet was not there.

And how did Lady Gaster's party go?
Juliet was next me and I do not know.

W. H. DAVIES
1871–1940
The Visitor

She brings that breath, and music too,
　　That comes when April's days begin;
And sweetness Autumn never had
　　In any bursting skin.

She's big with laughter at the breasts,
　　Like netted fish they leap:
Oh God, that I were far from here,
　　Or lying fast asleep!

WALTER DE LA MARE
1873–1956

Alone

The abode of the nightingale is bare,
Flowered frost congeals in the gelid air,
The fox howls from his frozen lair:
   Alas, my loved one is gone,
   I am alone:
   It is winter.

Once the pink cast a winy smell,
The wild bee hung in the hyacinth bell,
Light in effulgence of beauty fell:
   Alas, my loved one is gone,
   I am alone:
   Is is winter.

My candle a silent fire doth shed,
Starry Orion hunts o'erhead;
Come moth, come shadow, the world is dead:
   Alas, my loved one is gone,
   I am alone;
   It is winter.

EDWARD THOMAS
1878–1917

The Unknown

She is most fair,
And when they see her pass
The poet's ladies
Look no more in the glass
But after her.

On a bleak moor
Running under the moon
She lures a poet,
Once proud or happy, soon
Far from his door.

Beside a train,
Because they saw her go,
Or failed to see her,
Travellers and watchers know
Another pain.

The simple lack
Of her is more to me
Than others' presence,
Whether life splendid be
Or utter black.

I have not seen,
I have no news of her;
I can tell only
She is not here, but there
She might have been.

She is to be kissed
Only perhaps by me;
She may be seeking
Me and no other; she
May not exist.

No One So Much As You

No one so much as you
Loves this my clay,
Or would lament as you
Its dying day.

You know me through and through
Though I have not told,
And though with what you know
You are not bold.

None ever was so fair
As I thought you:
Not a word can I bear
Spoken against you.

All that I ever did
For you seemed coarse
Compared with what I hid
Nor put in force.

My eyes scarce dare meet you
Lest they should prove
I but respond to you
And do not love.

We look and understand,
We cannot speak –
Except in trifles and
Words the most weak.

For I at most accept
Your love, regretting
That is all: I have kept
Only a fretting

That I could not return
All that you gave
And could not ever burn
With the love you have,

Till sometimes it did seem
Better it were
Never to see you more
Than linger here

With only gratitude
Instead of love –
A pine in solitude
Cradling a dove.

HAROLD MONRO

1879–1932

The Terrible Door

Too long outside your door I have shivered.
You open it? I will not stay.
I'm haunted by your ashen beauty.
Take back your hand. I have gone away.

Don't talk, but move to that near corner.
I loathe the long cold shadow here.
We will stand a moment in the lamplight,
Until I watch you hard and near.

Happy release! Good-bye for ever!
Here at the corner we say good-bye.
But if you want me, if you do need me,
Who waits, at the terrible door, but I?

D. H. LAWRENCE

1885–1930

New Year's Eve

There are only two things now,
The great black night scooped out
And this fireglow.

This fireglow, the core,
And we the two ripe pips
That are held in store.

Listen, the darkness rings
As it circulates round our fire.
Take off your things.

Your shoulders, your bruised throat!
Your breasts, your nakedness!
This fiery coat!

As the darkness flickers and dips,
As the firelight falls and leaps
From your feet to your lips!

Green

The dawn was apple-green,
   The sky was green wine held up in the sun,
The moon was a golden petal between.

She opened her eyes, and green
   They shone, clear like flowers undone
For the first time, now for the first time seen.

Gloire de Dijon

When she rises in the morning
I linger to watch her;
She spreads the bath-cloth underneath the window
And the sunbeams catch her
Glistening white on the shoulders,
While down her sides the mellow
Golden shadow glows as
She stoops to the sponge, and her swung breasts
Sway like full-blown yellow
Gloire de Dijon roses.

She drips herself with water, and her shoulders
Glisten as silver, they crumple up
Like wet and falling roses, and I listen
For the sluicing of their rain-dishevelled petals.
In the window full of sunlight
Concentrates her golden shadow
Fold on fold, until it glows as
Mellow as the glory roses.

RUPERT BROOKE
1887–1915

Safety

Dear! of all happy in the hour, most blest
  He who has found our hid security,
Assured in the dark tides of the world that rest,
  And heard our word, 'Who is so safe as we?'
We have found safety with all things undying,
  The winds, and morning, tears of men and mirth,
The deep night, and birds singing, and clouds flying,
  And sleep, and freedom, and the autumnal earth.

We have built a house that is not for Time's throwing.
  We have gained a peace unshaken by pain for ever.
War knows no power. Safe shall be my going,
  Secretly armed against all death's endeavour;
Safe though all safety's lost; safe where men fall;
  And if these poor limbs die, safest of all.

The Hill

Breathless, we flung us on the windy hill,
Laughed in the sun, and kissed the lovely grass.
You said, 'Through glory and ecstasy we pass;
Wind, sun, and earth remain, the birds sing still,
When we are old, are old....' 'And when we die
All's over that is ours; and life burns on
Through other lovers, other lips,' said I,
'Heart of my heart, our heaven is now, is won!'

'We are Earth's best, that learnt her lesson here.
Life is our cry. We have kept the faith!' we said;
'We shall go down with unreluctant tread
Rose-crowned into the darkness!'. . . Proud we were,
And laughed, that had such brave true things to say.
– And then you suddenly cried, and turned away.

Lust

How should I know? The enormous wheels of will
    Drove me cold-eyed on tired and sleepless feet.
Night was void arms and you a phantom still,
    And day your far light swaying down the street.
As never fool for love, I starved for you;
    My throat was dry and my eyes hot to see.
Your mouth so lying was most heaven to view,
    And your remembered smell most agony.

Love wakens love! I felt your hot wrist shiver,
    And suddenly the mad victory I planned
        Flashed real, in your burning bending head . . .
My conqueror's blood was cool as a deep river
    In shadow; and my heart beneath your hand
        Quieter than a dead man on a bed.

ISAAC ROSENBERG

1890–1918

You and I

You and I have met but for an instant;
And no word the gate-lips let from out them.
But the eyes, voice audible – the soul's lips,
Stirr'd the depths of thought and feeling in me.

I have seen you somewhere, some sweet sometime,
Somewhere in a dim-remembered sometime.
Was it in the sleep-spun realm of dreamland?
In sweet woods, a faery flower of fancy?

If our hands touched would it bring us nearer?
As our souls touched, eyes' flame meeting eyes' flame.
If the lips spake would it lift the curtain
More than our mute bearing unaffected
Told the spirit's secrets eloquently?

Strange! this vast and universal riddle!
How perplexing! Manifold the wonder.
You and I, we meet but for an instant,
Pause or pass, reflections in a mirror.
And I see myself and wonder at it.
See myself in you, a double wonder.
With my thought held in a richer casket,
Clothed and girt in shape of regal beauty.
Strange! we pause! New waves of life rush blindly,
Madly on the soul's dumb silent breakers.

And a music strange is new awakened.
Fate the minstrel smites or holds the chord back.
Smites – new worlds undreamt of burst upon us.
All our life before was but embryo
Shaping for this birth – this living moment.

JOHN PEALE BISHOP
1892-1944

Metamorphoses of M

I

I have seen your feet gilded by morning
Naked under your long gown. I have seen them
Keep such state upon the unswept floor
I could have sworn Venetian artisans
Had all night been awake, painting in gold,
To set your beauty on appropriate heels.
What wonder then that I insist on gilt
As covering for your feet, which might inlay
(If there were still such metamorphoses)
The morning and form a constellation
To take all eyes from Venus, though she stood
As from antiquity in naked light
Till then unvying queen.

II

Your beauty is not used. Though you have lain
A thousand nights upon my bed, you rise
Always so splendidly renewed that I have thought,
Seeing the sweet continence of your breast,
Mole-spotted, your small waist, and long slim thigh,
That even the unicorn that savage beast.
If he should startle on you fresh from light
Would be so marvelled by virginity
That he would come, trotting and mild
To lay his head upon your fragrant lap
And be surprised.

EDNA ST VINCENT MILLAY

1892–1950

Sonnet 41

I, being born a woman and distressed
By all the needs and notions of my kind,
Am urged by your propinquity to find
Your person fair, and feel a certain zest
To bear your body's weight upon my breast:
So subtly is the fume of life designed,
To clarify the pulse and cloud the mind,
And leave me once again undone, possessed.
Think not for this, however, the poor treason
Of my stout blood against my staggering brain,
I shall remember you with love, or season
My scorn with pity, – let me make it plain:
I find this frenzy insufficient reason
For conversation when we meet again.

WILFRED OWEN

1893–1918

Greater Love

Red lips are not so red
  As the stained stones kissed by the English dead.
Kindness of wooed and wooer
Seems shame to their love pure.
O Love, your eyes lose lure
  When I behold eyes blinded in my stead!

Your slender attitude
  Trembles not exquisite like limbs knife-skewed,
Rolling and rolling there
Where God seems not to care;
Till the fierce Love they bear
  Cramps them in death's extreme decrepitude.

Your voice sings not so soft,–
Though even as wind murmuring through raftered loft,–
  Your dear voice is not dear,
Gentle, and evening clear,
As theirs whom none now hear,
  Now earth has stopped their piteous mouths that coughed.

Heart, you were never hot,
  Nor large, nor full like hearts made great with shot;
And though your hand be pale,
Paler are all which trail
Your cross through flame and hail:
  Weep, you may weep, for you may touch them not.

DOROTHY PARKER

1893–1967

One Perfect Rose

A single flow'r he sent me, since we met.
    All tenderly his messenger he chose;
Deep-hearted, pure, with scented dew still wet –
    One perfect rose.

I knew the language of the floweret;
    'My fragile leaves', it said, 'his heart enclose'.
Love long has taken for his amulet
    One perfect rose.

Why is it no one ever sent me yet
    One perfect limousine, do you suppose?
Ah no, it's always just my luck to get
    One perfect rose.

Social Note

Lady, lady, should you meet
One whose ways are all discreet,
One who murmurs that his wife
Is the lodestar of his life,
One who keeps assuring you
That he never was untrue,
Never loved another one ...
    Lady, lady, better run!

Unfortunate Coincidence

By the time you swear you're his,
    Shivering and sighing,
And he vows his passion is
    Infinite, undying—
Lady, make a note of this:
    One of you is lying.

e. e. cummings
1894–1962

i like my body when it is with your

i like my body when it is with your
body. It is so quite new a thing.
Muscles better and nerves more.
i like your body. i like what it does,
i like its hows. i like to feel the spine
of your body and its bones, and the trembling
-firm-smooth ness and which i will
again and again and again
kiss, i like kissing this and that of you,
i like, slowly stroking the, shocking fuzz
of your electric fur, and what-is-it comes
over parting flesh . . . And eyes big love-crumbs,

and possibly i like the thrill

of under me you so quite new

ROBERT GRAVES

1895-1985

The Thieves

Lovers in the act dispense
With such meum-tuum sense
As might warningly reveal
What they must not pick or steal,
And their nostrum is to say:
'I and you are both away.'

After, when they disentwine
You from me and yours from mine,
Neither can be certain who
Was that I whose mine was you.
To the act again they go
More completely not to know.

Theft is theft and raid is raid
Though reciprocally made.
Lovers, the conclusion is
Doubled sighs and jealousies
In a single heart that grieves
For lost honour among thieves.

Symptoms Of Love

Love is a universal migraine,
A bright stain on the vision
Blotting out reason.

Symptoms of true love
Are leanness, jealousy,
Laggard dawns;

Are omens and nightmares–
Listening for a knock,
Waiting for a sign:

For a touch of her fingers
In a darkened room,
For a searching look.

Take courage, lover!
Can you endure such grief
At any hand but hers?

OGDEN NASH

1902–1971

To My Valentine

More than a catbird hates a cat,
Or a criminal hates a clue,
Or the Axis hates the United States,
That's how much I love you.

I love you more than a duck can swim,
And more than a grapefruit squirts,
I love you more than gin rummy is a bore,
And more than a toothache hurts.

As a shipwrecked sailor hates the sea,
Or a juggler hates a shove,
As a hostess detests unexpected guests,
That's how much you I love.

I love you more than a wasp can sting,
And more than the subway jerks,
I love you as much as a beggar needs a crutch,
And more than a hangnail irks.

I swear to you by the stars above,
And below, if such there be,
As the High Court loathes perjurious oaths,
That's how you're loved by me.

SIR JOHN BETJEMAN

1906–1984

A Subaltern's Love-song

Miss J. Hunter Dunn, Miss J. Hunter Dunn,
Furnish'd and burnish'd by Aldershot sun,
What strenuous singles we played after tea,
We in the tournament – you against me!

Love-thirty, love-forty, oh! weakness of joy,
The speed of a swallow, the grace of a boy,
With carefullest carelessness, gaily you won,
I am weak from your loveliness, Joan Hunter
   Dunn.

Miss Joan Hunter Dunn, Miss Joan Hunter
   Dunn,
How mad I am, sad I am, glad that you won.
The warm-handled racket is back in its press,
But my shock-headed victor, she loves me no less.

Her father's euonymus shines as we walk,
And swing past the summer-house, buried in talk,
And cool the verandah that welcomes us in
To the six-o'clock news and a lime-juice and gin.

The scent of the conifers, sound of the bath,
The view from my bedroom of moss-dappled
   path,
As I struggle with double-end evening tie,
For we dance at the Golf Club, my victor and I.

On the floor of her bedroom lie blazer and shorts
And the cream-coloured walls are be-trophied
  with sports,
And westering, questioning settles the sun
On your low-leaded window, Miss Joan Hunter
  Dunn.

The Hillman is waiting, the light's in the hall,
The pictures of Egypt are bright on the wall,
My sweet, I am standing beside the oak stair
And there on the landing's the light on your hair.

By roads "not adopted", by woodlanded ways,
She drove to the club in the late summer haze,
Into nine-o'clock Camberley, heavy with bells
And mushroomy, pine-woody, evergreen smells.

Miss Joan Hunter Dunn, Miss Joan Hunter
  Dunn,
I can hear from the car-park the dance has begun.
Oh! full Surrey twilight! importunate band!
Oh! strongly adorable tennis-girl's hand!

Around us are Rovers and Austins afar,
Above us, the intimate roof of the car,
And here on my right is the girl of my choice,
With the tilt of her nose and the chime of her
  voice,

And the scent of her wrap, and the words never
  said,
And the ominous, ominous dancing ahead.
We sat in the car park till twenty to one
And now I'm engaged to Miss Joan Hunter
  Dunn.

Myfanwy

Kind o'er the *kinderbank* leans my Myfanwy,
   White o'er the play-pen the sheen of her dress,
Fresh from the bathroom and soft in the nursery
   Soap-scented fingers I long to caress.

Were you a prefect and head of your dormit'ry?
   Were you a hockey girl, tennis or gym?
Who was your favourite? Who had a crush on you?
   Which were the baths where they taught you to swim?

Smooth down the Avenue glitters the bicycle,
   Black-stockinged legs under navy-blue serge,
Home and Colonial, Star, International,
   Balancing bicycle leant on the verge.

Trace me your wheel-tracks, you fortunate bicycle,
   Out of the shopping and into the dark.
Back down the Avenue, back to the pottingshed,
   Back to the house on the fringe of the park.

Golden the light on the locks of Myfanwy,
   Golden the light on the book on her knee,
Finger-marked pages of Rackham's Hans Andersen.
   Time for the children to come down to tea.

Oh! Fuller's angel-cake, Robertson's marmalade,
   Liberty lampshade, come, shine on us all.
My! what a spread for the friends of Myfanwy
   Some in the alcove and some in the hall.

Then what sardines in the half-lighted passages!
   Locking of fingers in long hide-and-seek.
You will protect me, my silken Myfanwy,
   Ringleader, tom-boy, and chum to the weak.

In A Bath Teashop

'Let us not speak, for the love we bear one another—
  Let us hold hands and look.'
She, such a very ordinary little woman;
  He, such a thumping crook:
But both, for the moment, little lower than the angels
  In the teashop inglenook.

W. H. AUDEN
1907–1973
Lullaby

Lay your sleeping head, my love,
Human on my faithless arm;
Time and fevers burn away
Individual beauty from
Thoughtful children, and the grave
Proves the child ephemeral:
But in my arms till break of day
Let the living creature lie,
Mortal, guilty, but to me
The entirely beautiful.

Soul and body have no bounds:
To lovers as they lie upon
Her tolerant enchanted slope
In their ordinary swoon,
Grave the vision Venus sends
Of supernatural sympathy,
Universal love and hope;
While an abstract insight wakes
Among the glaciers and the rocks
The hermit's carnal ecstasy.

Certainty, fidelity
On the stroke of midnight pass
Like vibrations of a bell
And fashionable madmen raise
Their pedantic boring cry:
Every farthing of the cost,
All the dreaded cards foretell,
Shall be paid, but from this night
Not a whisper, not a thought,
Not a kiss nor look be lost.

Beauty, midnight, vision dies:
Let the winds of dawn that blow
Softly round your dreaming head
Such a day of welcome show
Eye and knocking heart may bless,
Find our mortal world enough;
Noons of dryness find you fed
By the involuntary powers,
Nights of insult let you pass
Watched by every human love.

PAUL DEHN

1912–1976

At The Dark Hour

Our love was conceived in silence and must live silently.
This only our sorrow, and this until the end.
Listen, did we not lie all of one evening,
Your heart under my hand

And no word spoken, no, not even the sighing
Of pain made comfortable, not the heart's beat
Nor sound of urgency, but a fire dying
And the cold sheet?

The sailor goes home singing; the lamplit lovers
Make private movements in a public place.
Boys whistle under windows, and are answered;
But we must hold our peace.

Day, too, broke silently. Before the blackbird,
Before the trouble of traffic and the mist unrolled,
I shall remember at the dark hour turning to you
For comfort in the cold.

JUDITH WRIGHT

1915–

The Company Of Lovers

We meet and part now over all the world.
We, the lost company,
take hands together in the night, forget
the night in our brief happiness, silently.
We who sought many things, throw all away
for this one thing, one only,
remembering that in the narrow grave
we shall be lonely.

Death marshals up his armies round us now.
Their footsteps crowd too near.
Lock your warm hand above the chilling heart
and for a time I live without my fear.
Grope in the night to find me and embrace,
for the dark preludes of the drums begin,
and round us, round the company of lovers,
Death draws his cordons in.

ALUN LEWIS

1915–1944

Goodbye

So we must say Goodbye, my darling,
And go, as lovers go, for ever;
Tonight remains, to pack and fix on labels
And make an end of lying down together.

I put a final shilling in the gas,
And watch you slip your dress below your knees
And lie so still I hear your rustling comb
Modulate the autumn in the trees.

And all the countless things I shall remember
Lay mummy-cloths of silence round my head;
I fill the carafe with a drink of water;
You say 'We paid a guinea for this bed,'

And then, 'We'll leave some gas, a little warmth
For the next resident, and these dry flowers,'
And turn your face away, afraid to speak
The big word, that Eternity is ours.

Your kisses close my eyes and yet you stare
As though God struck a child with nameless fears;
Perhaps the water glitters and discloses
Time's chalice and its limpid useless tears.

Everything we renounce except our selves;
Selfishness is the last of all to go;
Our sighs are exhalations of the earth,
Our footprints leave a track across the snow.

We made the universe to be our home,
Our nostrils took the wind to be our breath,
Our hearts are massive towers of delight,
We stride across the seven seas of death.

Yet when all's done you'll keep the emerald
I placed upon your finger in the street;
And I will keep the patches that you sewed
On my old battledress tonight, my sweet.

ALEX COMFORT

1920–

Love Poem

There is a white mare that my love keeps
unridden in a hillside meadow – white
as a white pebble, veined like a stone
a white horse, whiter than a girl

And now for three nights sleeping I have seen
her body naked as a tree for marriage
pale as a stone that the net of water covers

And her veined breasts like hills – the swallow islands
still on the corn's green water: and I know
her dark hairs gathered round an open rose

her pebbles lying under the dappled sea.
And I will ride her thighs' white horses.

HOWARD MOSS

1922–1987

Rain

Dear, on a day of dumb rain,
When cats sleep and trees grow,
And, outside the windowpane,
Imaginary fish flow,
We, as lovers, lace our arms
Securely round each other's back,
Hoping to stave off lightning's harm,
To counter thunder's crack.

Then pleasure is as easy as
The body's closeness, and the mind's;
There is a kind of love that has
Them separate, but body finds
Body too tasteless without thought,
And lovers feel, when face to face,
That mere intellect falls short,
Short of an embrace.

Dwindling, the slim rain makes us seem
As green as any world that grows;
Intransitive in sleep, we dream
Ourselves curled tightly as the rose,
Whose bud we cannot praise too much:
This is the start of every song
That no philosophy can touch—
And only the dead are wrong.

KINGSLEY AMIS

1922–

An Ever-Fixed Mark

Years ago, at a private school
Run on traditional lines,
One fellow used to perform
Prodigious feats in the dorm:
His quite undevious designs
Found many a willing tool.

On the rugger field, in the gym,
Buck marked down at his leisure
The likeliest bits of stuff;
The notion, familiar enough,
Of "using somebody for pleasure"
Seemed handy and harmless to him.

But another chap was above
The diversions of such a lout.
Seven years in the place
And he never got to first base
With the kid he followed about.
What interested Ralph was love.

He did the whole thing in style:
Letters three times a week,
Sonnet-sequences, Sunday walks.

At last, during one of their talks,
The youngster caressed his cheek,
And that made it all worth while.

Nowadays, for a quid pro quo,
Ralph's chum does what, and with which;
Buck's playmates, family men,
Eye a Boy Scout now and then.
Sex is a momentary itch,
Love never lets you go.

ALAN ROSS
1922–

In Bloemfontein

Woman to man, they lie,
He not quite white
As she, nor she
So black as he.

Save where her stomach curves
His flesh and hers,
Commingling, match.
Eyes catch,

That dare not meet
Beyond the night,
Though their alternate
Thighs, locked tight,

Defy you to discriminate
Between his skin and hers.
To him Pass Laws
Apply; she knows no night.

But that pale stripe her loins
Keep from the sun
Marks her, his tiger-woman,
White, while he's all one.

That stripe convicts. He covers
With his hand the site
Of crime. Soon shutters,
Striping him with light

Peel colour from his hips –
She his woman, he
Her man, simply human
Like the heart beneath her lips.

A matter of degree
Elsewhere, no more;
But here, in Bloemfontein,
Keep closed the door.

PHILIP LARKIN
1923–1985

Talking In Bed

Talking in bed ought to be easiest,
Lying together there goes back so far,
An emblem of two people being honest.

Yet more and more time passes silently.
Outside, the wind's incomplete unrest
Builds and disperses clouds about the sky,

And dark towns heap up on the horizon.
None of this cares for us. Nothing shows why
At this unique distance from isolation

It becomes still more difficult to find
Words at once true and kind,
Or not untrue and not unkind.

Lines On A Young Lady's Photograph Album

At last you yielded up the album, which,
Once open, sent me distracted. All your ages
Matt and glossy on the thick black pages!
Too much confectionery, too rich:
I choke on such nutritious images.

My swivel eye hungers from pose to pose—
In pigtails, clutching a reluctant cat;
Or furred yourself, a sweet girl-graduate;
Or lifting a heavy-headed rose
Beneath a trellis, or in a trilby hat

(Faintly disturbing, that, in several ways)—
From every side you strike at my control,
Not least through these disquieting chaps who loll
At ease about your earlier days:
Not quite your class, I'd say, dear, on the whole.

But O, photography! as no art is,
Faithful and disappointing! that records
Dull days as dull, and hold-it smiles as frauds,
And will not censor blemishes
Like washing-lines, and Hall's-Distemper boards,

But shows the cat was disinclined, and shades
A chin as doubled when it is, what grace
Your candour thus confers upon her face!
How overwhelmingly persuades
That this is a real girl in a real place,

In every sense empirically true!
Or is it just *the past?* Those flowers, that grate,
These misty parks and moors, lacerate
Simply by being over; you
Contract my heart by looking out of date.

Yes, true; but in the end, surely, we cry
Not only at exclusion, but because
It leaves us free to cry. We know *what was*
Won't call on us to justify
Our grief, however hard we yowl across

The gap from eye to page. So I am left
To mourn (without a chance of consequence)
You, balanced on a bike against a fence;
To wonder if you'd spot the theft
Of this one of you bathing; to condense,

In short, a past that no one now can share,
No matter whose your future; calm and dry,
It holds you like a heaven, and you lie
Unvariably lovely there,
Smaller and clearer as the years go by.

BARRIE REID

1926–

Sonnet

Love don't be lonely, you are not clear water
to remember only loss when midnight and faraway
move torment and lover together in the air
until the persistent rains blot out all the bright day
the bright day where you and the gay birds were.

Lovers are more than mirrors, moving or still,
and are the house and the enfolding trees
and are the lovely distance and the hill
and Jack Brighteyes and all the world he sees.

If you are love then you are all the world,
though in this world murder will find no prey
prey no murder, the beast will tear at his eyes,
if midnight tears the lover from his love's bright day
and moves him blindfold under distant skies.

ROBERT CREELEY

1926–

The Way

My love's manners in bed
are not to be discussed by me,
as mine by her
I would not credit comment upon gracefully.

Yet I ride by the margin of that lake in
the wood, the castle,
and the excitement of strongholds;
and have a small boy's notion of doing good.

Oh well, I will say here,
knowing each man,
let you find a good wife too,
and love her as hard as you can.

CHARLES OSBORNE

1927–

A Pop Song For Sadie

If you were a flower, you'd be a crimson rosebud,
If you were a bird, a cooing turtle-dove,
If you were a poem, you'd be by Keats or Shelley,
a colour, silver as the moon above.

If you were to eat, you'd be a bowl of cherries,
a month, you'd be the sunny days of June,
If you were a singer, you'd be Judy Garland,
If you were a song, then Gershwin wrote your tune.

If you were a planet, you'd be none but Venus,
If you were a waltz, you'd be the best of Strauss,
If you were a city, you'd be San Francisco,
a cartoon character, you're Minnie Mouse.

If you were a boy, I'd change my sex for you, dear,
If you were a ghost, I'd die, to be one, too,
If you were a dream, I'd hope never to waken,
So thank Christ, sweetheart, you are only you.

PETER PORTER

1929–

Beast And The Beauty

His fear never loud in daylight, risen to a night whisper
Of a dead mother in the weatherboard house,
He had this great piece of luck: a girl
In Paris clothes, ex-school monitor, chose
Him for her lover. Twenty-one and experienced,
She showed his hands the presentiment of clothes
And first at a party kissed him, then took
Him home where they did what he'd always supposed.

Her sophistication was his great delight:
Her mother and father drinking, throwing things,
The unhappy marriage, the tradespeople on Christian
Name terms – all the democratic sexiness – mornings
With the Pick of the Pops and the Daily Express
And yet the sudden itching despair, the wonder in King's
College Chapel, the depth that lived in her soul
Of which this raciness was only the worldly covering.

But the sophistication chose to kill – the itch
Was on the inside of the skin. Her family of drunks
Were shrewd, wine-wise young barristers and gentlemen-
Farmers fought for her hand. In the loft there waited trunks
Of heirlooms to be taken seriously. He found himself
Ditched, his calls unanswered, his world shrunk
To eating in Lyons', waiting outside her house at midnight,
Her serious tears to haunt him, boiling on his bunk.

So he sits alone in Libraries, hideous and hairy of soul,
A beast again, waiting for a lustful kiss to bring
Back his human smell, the taste of woman on his tongue.

RAY MATHEW

1929–

Young Man's Fancy

Come tomorrow night,
or don't come ever.
The moon will give light
enough for a lover.

I'll stand in the deep dark
of a gum-tree's shadow,
but you'll find me all right
if you really want to.

But I won't wait long,
You must come if you're coming.
Without talk of wrong
or breakfast at morning.

If they find out
just say you were walking
to see if the night
could stop a head aching.

And don't mention me
because I don't own you.
We just happen to meet;
I don't really know you.

Yes, I want you to come,
with the moon in your hair.
And the moon in your eyes
as you look for me there.

Yes, I want you to come,
but I'll promise you nothing.
And if you're not game
then I still won't be crying.

But come tomorrow night
or don't come ever.
I won't spend two nights
waiting for a lover.

TED HUGHES
1930–

September

We sit late, watching the dark slowly unfold:
No clock counts this.
When kisses are repeated and the arms hold
There is no telling where time is.

It is midsummer: the leaves hang big and still:
Behind the eye a star,
Under the silk of the wrist a sea, tell
Time is nowhere.

We stand; leaves have not timed the summer.
No clock now needs
Tell we have only what we remember:
Minutes uproaring with our heads

Like an unfortunate King's and his Queen's
When the senseless mob rules;
And quietly the trees casting their crowns
Into the pools.

THE END

ACKNOWLEDGMENTS

The editor gratefully acknowledges permission to reproduce copyright poems in this book.

KINGSLEY AMIS: 'An Ever-Fixed Mark' from *A Look Round the Estate*. Copyright © 1967 Kingsley Amis. Reprinted by permission of Jonathan Clowes Ltd, London, on behalf of Kingsley Amis.

W. H. AUDEN: 'Lullaby' from *Collected Poems*. Reprinted by permission of Faber & Faber Ltd.

HILAIRE BELLOC: 'Juliet' from *Sonnets and Verse* (Gerald Duckworth & Co. Ltd). Reprinted by permission of A. D. Peters and Company Ltd.

JOHN BETJEMAN: 'A Subaltern's Love', 'Myfanwy', and 'In a Bath Teashop' from *Collected Poems*. Reprinted by permission of John Murray (Publishers) Ltd.

JOHN PEALE BISHOP: 'Metamorphoses of M' from *Selected Poems*. Reprinted by permission of Charles Scribner's Sons, New York.

ALEX COMFORT: 'Love Poem' from *Haste to the Wedding*. Reproduced by permission of David Higham Associates Ltd.

ROBERT CREELEY: 'The Way' from *The Poems of Robert Creeley 1950–1965*. Reproduced by permission of Marion Boyars Publishers Ltd.

E. E. CUMMINGS: 'i like my body when it is with your'. Reproduced by permission of the Liveright Publishing Corp., Inc.

W. H. DAVIES: 'The Visitor' from *The Complete Poems of W. H. Davies*. Reprinted by permission of Jonathan Cape Ltd on behalf of the Executors of the W. H. Davies Estate.

PAUL DEHN: 'At the Dark Hour' from *The Fern on the Rock* (1965). Reprinted by permission of Dehn Enterprises Ltd, London.

WALTER DE LA MARE: 'Alone'. Reprinted by permission of the Literary Trustees of Walter de la Mare, and the Society of Authors as their representative.

ROBERT GRAVES: 'Symptoms of Love' and 'The Thieves'. Reproduced by permission of Cassell plc, London.

TED HUGHES: 'September' from *The Hawk in the Rain*. Reprinted by permission of Faber & Faber Ltd.

PHILIP LARKIN: 'Talking in Bed' from *The Whitsun Weddings*. Reprinted by permission of Faber & Faber Ltd, London. 'Lines on a Young Lady's Photograph Album' from *The Less Deceived*. Reproduced by permission of The Marvell Press, England.

ALUN LEWIS: 'Goodbye' from *Ha Ha Among the Trumpets*. Reprinted by permission of Unwin Hyman Ltd.

RAY MATHEW: 'Young Man's Fancy'. Reproduced by permission of Ray Mathew.

HOWARD MOSS: 'Rain'. Reprinted by permission of the Estate of Howard Moss.

OGDEN NASH: 'To My Valentine'. Reproduced by permission of André Deutsch.

CHARLES OSBORNE: 'A Pop Song for Sadie'. Reprinted by permission of Charles Osborne.

DOROTHY PARKER: 'Social Note', 'Unfortunate Coincidence' and 'One Perfect Rose' from *The Collected Dorothy Parker*. Reprinted by permission of Gerald Duckworth.

PETER PORTER: 'Beast and the Beauty' from *Collected Poems* (1983). Copyright © Peter Porter 1983. Reprinted by permission of Oxford University Press.

BARRIE REID: 'Sonnet'. Reproduced by permission of Barrie Reid.

ALAN ROSS: 'In Bloemfontein'. Reproduced by permission of Alan Ross.

EDNA ST VINCENT MILLAY: 'I, being born a woman and distressed' from *Collected Poems*. Copyright © 1923, 1951 by Edna St Vincent Millay and Norma Millay Ellis. Reprinted by permission.

JUDITH WRIGHT: 'The Company of Lovers' from *Selected Poems*, *Five Senses* by Judith Wright. Reproduced by permission of Angus & Robertson (UK).

WILLIAM BUTLER YEATS: 'Brown Penny', 'When You Are Old' and 'The Ragged Wood' from *The Collected Poems of W. B. Yeats*. Reprinted by permission of A. P. Watt Ltd on behalf of Michael B. Yeats and Macmillan London Ltd.

ANDREW YOUNG: 'Song for Autumn' from *The Poetical Works of Andrew Young*. Reprinted by permission of Martin Secker & Warburg Ltd.